Authority In Three Worlds

by
Charles Capps

I0681408

HARRISON HOUSE
Tulsa, Oklahoma

18th Printing

Authority in Three Worlds
ISBN 0-89274-281-X
Copyright © 1980, 1982 by Charles Capps
P. O. Box 69
England, Arkansas 72045
(formerly ISBN 0-89274-160-0)

Published by Harrison House, Inc.
P. O. Box 35035
Tulsa, Oklahoma 74153

Contents

Introduction

The phone rang in a business office and was very promptly answered. The angry voice on the line said, "I want to talk with someone around there with a little authority."

To that, the man replied, "Well, talk to me. I have about as little authority as anyone around here!"

This is too often the case with many believers today. They see themselves with such little authority that they wouldn't dare exercise it.

Authority In Three Worlds is dedicated to the Body of Christ. It is not intended to perpetrate a doctrine or stir any controversy. It simply brings together a whole picture of which so many have only a small part.

I challenge you to read it with an open mind and with much prayer. It is not a book you can read quickly. It requires some pauses for thought, meditation, and searching of Scriptures.

This book may come as a shock to the religious mind. Don't read it with your religious eyeglasses on, for this book will take you on a scriptural journey that will shock the average churchgoer.

It will cause sinners and saints alike to both weep and laugh for joy over so great a deliverance that was won for us by the holy Son of God.

Thousands will be saved while reading this book. Multitudes will be healed as the revelation of total deliverance unfolds in the pages of the Old Testament types.

Authority In Three Worlds is a scriptural help to a proverbial jigsaw puzzle. It will give you a wide-angle view of God's love and concern for man on earth and will cause you to fall deeply in love with Jesus, His Son.

1
Man Under Authority

The people of the world have not yet seen the authority given them through Jesus Christ. Neither have they accepted the authority that is rightfully theirs because of being born on earth.

Man was created in God's likeness to have fellowship with Deity. *He was the crown of all creation.* He possessed abilities beyond our comprehension, yet he failed because he broke God's Word. When Adam bowed his knee to Satan, he lost his spiritual authority.

Let's begin with Matthew 8:5-10 and use this as a launching point into authority.

And when Jesus was entered into Capernaum, there came unto him a centurion, beseeching him, and saying, Lord, my servant lieth at home sick of the palsy, grievously tormented.

And Jesus saith unto him, I will come and heal him.

The centurion answered and said, Lord, I am not worthy that thou shouldest come under my roof: but speak the word only, and my servant shall be healed.

For I am a man under authority, having soldiers under me: and I say to this man, Go, and he goeth; and to another, Come, and he cometh; and to my servant, Do this, and he doeth it.

When Jesus heard it, he marvelled, and said to them that followed, Verily I say unto you, I have not found so great faith, no, not in Israel.

This man was a Gentile. He was not a Covenant man. He was an outcast in his day and had no legal grounds to come to Jesus. The Gospel was to the Jew first, then to the Gentile. Even when Jesus sent His disciples to preach, He said, "Go to those of the House of Israel. Go not into the way of the Gentile." (Matt. 10:5,6.)

This man was not included in the Covenant, but Jesus said, "I will come and heal your servant." The centurion told Jesus that He didn't have to walk to his house. In those days, Jesus couldn't catch a plane or a train. He either had to walk or ride a donkey, and if you've ever been on one of those donkeys, you know that you would rather walk!

The centurion said to Jesus, "You don't have to walk to my house, for I'm a man under authority and I know how authority works. When I'm told to do something, I do it. I have soldiers under me, and when I tell them to come or go, they do it. Now, You just *speak the word* and my servant shall be healed."

This is the highest form of faith.

I asked the Lord, "Why did the centurion have that kind of faith even though he was not included in the Covenant?"

The Lord said, "He was a military man who understood authority because he was under authority. If you will teach My people to understand authority as this man understood authority, *they will operate in the same kind of faith.*"

When you understand authority as the Bible sets it forth, you will rise to a new level of faith. *You will rise to an understanding of God's Word that will set you free from the circumstances of life!*

You can use your God-given authority by speaking His Word against the circumstances of life. They will conform to God's Word! The knowledge of this truth will set you free!

Take Authority Over Circumstances

One fellow met another and asked, "How are you doing?"

He replied, "Well, not so good under the circumstances."

The man said, "What are you doing *under* the circumstances?"

We have sung songs of unbelief for so long that we have begun to believe them! "I'm just a weary pilgrim, trudging through this world."

We are *not* weary pilgrims, trudging through this world! We were foreigners and strangers, but now *we are joint-heirs with Christ Jesus!*

Another song goes like this: "I know not today what tomorrow may bring—shadows or sunshine or rain." As you get an understanding of your authority through the Word of God, you won't have to worry about what tomorrow brings.

Take your faith and change what tomorrow brings!

The Knowledge of God

Jesus spoke a profound truth when He said, *If ye continue in my word, then are ye my disciples indeed; and ye shall know the truth, and the truth shall make you free* (John 8:31,32).

God spoke through His prophet Hosea, saying, *My people are destroyed for lack of knowledge: because thou hast rejected knowledge, I will also reject thee* (Hos. 4:6).

Solomon said, *For the Lord giveth wisdom: out of his mouth cometh knowledge and understanding* (Prov. 2:6).

One of the greatest needs of this day is to realize what God has done for us in Christ Jesus. We find insight to this in 2 Peter 1:1. *Simon Peter, a servant and an apostle of Jesus Christ, to them that have obtained like precious faith with us through the righteousness of God and our Saviour Jesus Christ.*

You will notice Peter is writing to *those* who have obtained like precious faith *with us.* In other words, you and I are included! We have obtained that same faith.

Grace and peace be multiplied unto you through the knowledge of God, and of Jesus our Lord (v. 2).

I want you to pay particular attention to the phrase, *the knowledge of God.* Grace and peace is *multiplied,* not *added,* to you! People are seeking for peace today. Most of them are seeking peace in places where it isn't found.

Notice, peace is multiplied to us through the knowledge of God and through the knowledge of Jesus, our Lord.

According as his divine power hath given unto us all things that pertain unto life and godliness, through the knowledge of him that hath called us to glory and virtue (v. 3).

If you have been given *all things,* there's just not any more He can give.

This scripture does *not* say, "He is going to give us all things, sometime." He has already done it! He has given us all things that pertain unto life and godliness through the knowledge of Him Who has called us to glory and virtue. *This comes only through the knowledge of God!*

The Word says:

And he gave some, apostles; and some, prophets; and some, evangelists; and some, pastors and teachers; for the perfecting of the saints, for the work of the ministry, for the edifying of the body of Christ:

Till we all come in the unity of the faith, and of the knowledge of the Son of God, unto a perfect man, unto the measure of the stature of the fulness of Christ.

Ephesians 4:11-13

He has given a fivefold ministry of apostles, prophets, evangelists, pastors, and teachers for the perfecting of the saints.

Truth Alone Won't Set You Free

Remember, Jesus' words to His disciples: *If ye continue in my word, then are ye my disciples indeed; and ye shall know the truth, and the truth shall make you free* (John 8:31,32).

I had been misquoting that. Then one day the Lord said to me, "That's not true."

I was shocked and said, "Well, You said it. It *must* be true."

He answered, "You aren't quoting *all* of it. *If ye continue in my word* . . . then you will know the truth, and the truth will make you free!"

Everyone won't know the truth because they're not continuing in the

Word. *It's the knowledge of the truth that sets you free!* **Many know *about* truth, but few have the knowledge *of* that truth.**

The Apostle Paul said, "All things **are** yours!" Peter said the same thing in 2 Peter 1, "The Lord **has already done it!**" He isn't **going to do it** some day. In fact, the Bible tells us, God finished His work in six days, then rested. Some of us have been trying to get God to work ever since! He set it all in motion. *It was accomplished in Jesus Christ and is available to all who will receive it.*

Freedom comes to us when we continue in God's Word because it produces the knowledge of God. Peter said, *According as his divine power . . . Whereby are given unto us exceeding great and precious promises: that by these ye might be partakers of the divine nature* (2 Pet. 1:3,4).

He didn't say you *had* to be partakers. He said you *might* be partakers. It's available to you. As partakers of God's nature, *you* are capable of operating on the same level of faith with God. Man was created to have fellowship with God, the Father.

2
In His Image

But one in a certain place testified, saying, What is man, that thou art mindful of him? or the son of man, that thou visitest him?

Thou madest him a little lower than the angels; thou crownedst him with glory and honour, and didst set him over the works of thy hands.

Hebrews 2:6,7

Notice, two different people are spoken of in these scriptures—man and the Son of Man. Jesus always called Himself "the Son of Man."

God set man over the work of His hands. **God gave man dominion over the earth!** *Thou madest him a little lower than the angels.*

The Greek states, ". . . for a little time, lower than the angels." Because of the Fall, man was made lower than the angels for a little while. Man was created on a higher order than angels in the beginning. Only man was given the right to choose his words and make his own decisions; the angels were not given that right.

Thou hast put all things in subjection under his feet. For in that he put all in subjection under him, he left nothing that is not put under him. But now we see not yet all things put under him.

Hebrews 2:8

If He put all things under him, there is no more to be put under him. He put all things in subjection under man's feet. As far as God is concerned, it was done when He put Adam over all things of this earth; Adam was given dominion over all the earth.

You can see in Genesis that man was created to have dominion. All things were put in subjection under his feet! God isn't going to do this for mankind, someday. He has already done it! God left nothing that was not put under man's feet! Man was put above it all.

You don't see all things put under him yet, but you do see Jesus Who was made like man. Man has not attained to that position because of Adam's fall, *but you see Jesus.*

Forasmuch then as the children are partakers of flesh and blood, he also himself likewise took part of the same; that through death he might destroy him that had the power of death, that is, the devil . . .

For verily he took not on him the nature of angels; but he took on him the seed of Abraham.

Wherefore in all things it behoved him to be made like unto his brethren, that he might be a merciful and faithful high priest in things pertaining to God, to make reconciliation for the sins of the people.

Hebrews 2:14,16,17

Jesus was made just like man. He took upon Himself the body of a man. He came to earth as a man and put all things under His feet.

Adam Was to be God Over the Earth

As you read about the creation of man in Genesis 1:26-28, you realize that mankind was created to rule the earth.

And God said, Let us make man in our image, after our likeness: and let them have dominion over the fish of the sea, and over the fowl of the air, and over the cattle, and

*over all the earth, and over every creeping
thing that creepeth upon the earth.*

*So God created man in his own image, in
the image of God created he him: male and
female created he them.*

*And God blessed them, and God said
unto them, Be fruitful, and multiply, and
replenish the earth, and subdue it: and have
dominion over the fish of the sea, and over
the fowl of the air, and over every living
thing that moveth upon the earth.*

Notice in verse 26 the word, *all—over
all the earth, and over every creeping thing
that creepeth upon the earth.*

Here is one of the most astounding
statements of the Bible: *Let us create man
in our image.*

*So God created man in his own image, in
the image of God created he him; male and
female created he them. And God blessed
them, and God said unto them, Be fruitful,
and multiply, and replenish the earth, and
subdue it . . .* (vv. 27,28).

It's important to notice that God did
not say, "Just be humble and let
circumstances of life bowl you over.
Don't ever do anything about your
circumstances. Just say, 'What is to

come will come' and do nothing to change it.''

No! God said, *Subdue it!* In other words, if the earth or any living creature gets out of line, *you* **put it back** in line! That's quite different from some of our Sunday school ideas.

God created man to be god over the earth. Man wasn't put here as a worm in the dust. God created the earth and gave it to him. It became man's to do with as he would, but God gave him some guidelines with the ability to carry them out.

The heaven, even the heavens, are the Lord's: but the earth hath he given to the children of men.

Psalm 115:16

God gave the earth to man. He said, ''If it gets out of line, don't call *Me. You* put it back in line.'' (That's 1 Capps 1:27). Don't lay down and play dead and say, ''Oh, I guess it's God's will.''

Use your faith and change the circumstances! Subdue it! Take dominion over it!

God said, *Let us make man in our image after our likeness.* The word

likeness in the original Hebrew means
"an exact duplication in kind."

God duplicated *Himself* in kind! Man
didn't spring from a monkey. He didn't
come from a single cell that decided to
crawl on the ground, then hang by its
tail from trees, and finally walk upright.
That's intellectual garbage!

God created man *full grown,* as god
over the earth. He gave this earth to
Adam and said, "Here it is, Adam. Be
god over the earth and everything in it.
If it gets out of line, *you* take care of it."

**Adam was *an exact duplication of
God's kind!*** He was created in the image
of his Creator. God created man after
His own kind. The whole law of
Genesis bears this out: Everything
produces after its kind. (See Gen. 1.)
God is a Spirit . . . (John 4:24).

You don't plant peaches to grow
oranges! You don't plant cucumbers and
harvest apples. Everything produces
after its kind. That's the law of
Genesis—the law of God.

God said as long as the earth
remained, there would be seedtime and
harvest, day and night, cold and heat; it
would never cease. (Gen. 8:22.) That

law is working. God's laws have never been superseded. They remain in effect today.

God created man after His likeness, an exact duplication in kind. Then, what *kind* is God? Jesus said, *God is a Spirit*. You aren't God. You aren't equal with God in His divine attributes, but you are a spirit being under authority. You are able to partake of God's divine nature: **righteousness.**

Adam was subordinate to God. God created him, gave him all this authority and power, and said to him, "Be god over the earth as I am God over the heavens."

The Bible tells us that man is created in the image and likeness of God. Man is a threefold being: He is a spirit; he has a soul; he lives in a body.

God said, *Let us make man in our image.* If man was made in God's image, then he is a triune being like God: the Father, the Son, and the Holy Ghost.

1. Man is a spirit. The human spirit contacts God, Who is a spirit.

2. The body relates to Jesus, Who was the physical manifestation of God in this earth.

3. The soul of man (which is composed of the will, the mind, and the emotions) relates to the Holy Spirit, Who is called Guide and Teacher.

I am convinced that the soul of man is the coupler that links the spirit to the body. The Holy Spirit is spoken of as *Guide* throughout the New Testament.

Since man was created an exact duplication of God's kind, he has to be a triune being in order to qualify for the likeness of God.

And Adam lived an hundred and thirty years, and begat a son in his own likeness, after his image; and called his name Seth (Gen. 5:3).

The exact words used to describe Adam's sons are used by God to describe man. Man was created in God's likeness and in His image. That's the law of Genesis. If everything produces after its kind, Seth had to look like Adam. Why would God deviate from His law of structure in the universe and create something that wasn't after God's kind? God stays with His law and uses the same words to describe Seth.

The Creation of Man

And the Lord God formed man of the dust of the ground, and breathed into his nostrils the breath of life; and man became a living soul (Gen. 2:7). Notice it said, "He *formed* man." This isn't the creation.

Some say man was created out of dust. That's not true.

Sometimes we have been like the little boy who heard his Sunday school teacher say, "We are made out of dust, and to dust we'll return."

The boy asked, "Did you say, 'We're made out of dust, and we're gonna turn back to dust?' "

"Yes, that's what God said."

The little boy replied, "Well, I looked under my desk, and there's somebody either coming or going!"

Some have been just as confused in their thinking concerning the creation of man.

The Bible shows that God *formed* man's body out of the dust of the earth. *Created* means "to bring into existence." **Forming something is not a creation.** You can take an existing substance and *form something*, but that isn't a creation.

You can construct a building from trees. The trees existed before the building was formed. The men didn't create the building. They built it—formed and fashioned it—from an already existing substance.

God took something He had already created (the earth) and formed man's body out of the dust of the already existing substance. There man was—complete with eyes, ears, nose, hands, feet—a perfect specimen. But he was as dead as a doornail. There was no life in him. If God had turned him loose, he would have fallen to the ground. There was no life in him until God breathed the breath of life into him. God breathed *His* life into Adam—**the life of God!**

And God blessed the seventh day, and sanctified it: because that in it he had rested from all his work which God created and made (Gen. 2:3).

God *created* some and *made* others. God *created* the earth, but He *made* man's body. He made it out of what He had already created, then He breathed life into that body—*spirit life!* The creation came when God breathed spirit life into Adam.

The word *spirit* means "wind or breath." God breathed His Spirit into man and man became an exact duplicate of God's kind.

3
Dominion Through Words

We see God's thought before and after the creation of man.

And God said, Let us make man in our image, after our likeness: and let them have dominion . . .

So God created man in his own image, in the image of God created he him; male and female created he them.

And God blessed them, and God said unto them . . . have dominion over the fish of the sea, and over the fowl of the air, and over every living thing that moveth upon the earth.

Genesis 1:26-28

How was Adam to subdue the earth?

As an exact duplication of God's own kind, Adam was capable of operating on the *same level of faith* with God. Adam was subordinate to God, but all of the earth was under his control. **Adam was a man under authority.**

Some think that God made the earth out of nothing, but He didn't. He made it out of something. **The substance God used was faith.**

Let's compare Genesis 1:1 with John 1:1.

In the beginning God . . . (Gen. 1:1).

In the beginning was the Word, and the Word was with God, and the Word was God (John 1:1).

Then John 1:3 says, *All things were made by him* (the Word); *and without him* (the Word) *was not any thing made that was made.* **God created the earth with words.**

God used His faith when He created. He releases His faith in His words. There was no light out there until God said, **"Light, be."** He produced light with His faith. He used His words as a carrier of that faith.

You'll find the words *And God said* spoken ten times in Genesis 1. Why didn't God tell Moses to write *And God said,* then list all the things God said?

The reason it was recorded this way was to reveal to you *how* God created.

He did it with words. He used His words as containers to carry His faith out where creation took place. God's words are filled with faith, and He used them to bring creation into existence.

Now faith is the substance of things hoped for . . . (Heb 11:1). Faith is the substance.

Some people think that the spirit world doesn't exist because they can't see it. But God, Who is a spirit, created this world!

Paul tells us to look at things that are *not seen.* How do you do that? *Through eyes of faith.*

Things that are seen are temporal, which means they are subject to change. We can see this world, so it is subject to change. It is *not* the established world. It will pass away.

The spirit world is the real world; it created all that you see. Genesis 1:1 states, *In the beginning God created . . . .* How? With the Word. There was nothing made without the Word. Jesus was the Word. Again, John 1:3 says, *All things were made by him; and without him was not any thing made that was made.*

Through faith we understand that the worlds were framed by the word of God, so that things which are seen were not made of things which do appear.

Hebrews 11:3

Things you see are not made with things which do appear. You can't see faith, but the world was made out of God's faith. *The things which are seen are temporal; but the things which are not seen are eternal* (2 Cor. 4:18). In other words, things you see are subject to change. That's why God told Adam to subdue the earth and have dominion over it. You can take your faith and change it!

Word of His Power

God, who at sundry times and in divers manners spake in time past unto the fathers by the prophets, hath in these last days spoken unto us by his Son, whom he hath appointed heir of all things, by whom also he made the worlds;

Who being the brightness of his glory, and the express image of his person, and upholding all things by the word of his power, when he had by himself purged our sins, sat down on the right hand of the Majesty on high.

Hebrews 1:1-3

Who being the brightness of his glory . . . . Whose glory? God's glory!

. . . the express image of his person . . . . Jesus is the express image of God's person. The Greek text states, "an exact expression of God's substance." If you want to know what God is like, look at Jesus. He said, *I and my Father are one* (John 10:30). He meant that He was the exact image, the express image of God's person.

Upholding all things by the word of his power . . . . If He had said, "by the power of His Word," then you could say there is *some* power in His Word, but not *all* power. But He didn't say that. He upholds all things by the Word of His power. **The spoken Word of God is *His power*.** It was His creative ability of words that released His faith.

Light travels at the speed of 186,000 miles per second. At the time of Creation, God called into existence more than 16 billion miles of universe within a twenty-four hour period!

Scientists say the universe is still expanding at the speed of light. There are galaxies beyond what we can see, millions of light-years away. (Distances in space are measured in light-years, which is the distance light travels in a year.) What a vast expanse God set in motion with His words!

God created Adam in His image and in His likeness. Adam was meant to have dominion over the earth by releasing his faith in words just as God had done with His. God used words to bring forth all creation. He set it in motion by saying, *Let there be . . .* (Gen. 1:3). **And there was!** God's faith was transported by words.

4
Keys to Understanding the Bible

The keys to understanding the Bible are in the first three chapters of Genesis. If you don't understand these chapters, you'll never be able to accurately understand the Bible. People today are atheists because they have not understood this important book of the Bible.

And God saw every thing that he had made, and behold, it was very good.

Genesis 1:31

God created after His kind, and everything He made was very good.

You may ask, "What about snakes and alligators?" God didn't create the animals as they are today. Animals didn't eat each other until after Noah put them out of the ark. (See Gen. 1:30; 9:1-5.)

Things we see on earth today are perversions of nature. They came about when Adam bowed his knee to the outlaw spirit and turned his authority over to Satan. Then Satan became god of the world system and perverted the things God had created.

Some say, "If there were a God, there wouldn't be all the wars and fighting. There wouldn't be trouble and turmoil. Little kids wouldn't be born crippled, and there wouldn't be all the suffering that is in the world today.' But there *is* a God—a God Who *keeps His Word*.

When Adam turned his authority over to Satan, Satan became the God of the world system. Through his wickedness, he set out to destroy God's creation. He perverted the nature of things God had created.

When you hear of a tornado destroying a city, invariably newspaper headlines describe it as "an act of God." Don't blame God! It was the Devil who visited that town!

When lightning struck an Arkansas plant, giant headlines read, **Act of God Kills 23, Injured Many More.** No bigger lie has ever been told. This is a perversion of nature.

Because of deception, many people think these evil things come from God. They read about Job and the things that came upon him, then come up with ideas foreign to the Bible. For example, Job 1:16 says, *The fire of God is fallen from heaven, and hath burned up the sheep, and the servants.* God didn't send it; the Devil sent it! The "fire" was lightning. The cattle were probably watering in a pond when lightning struck and killed them all. In that day, most people thought everything that happened came from God. This is why people are still confused in our day about things in the Old Testament.

We need to fully understand that God is our heavenly Father. He is *not* the perpetrator of death, evil, or calamity. The perversion was caused by the satanic forces turned loose on the earth.

Some have the idea that God sent death on man. But God is *not* the perpetrator of death; death is of the Devil. When Adam sinned, death came into the world. First Corinthians 15:21 tells us that death came by man.

God told Adam what would happen if he ate the forbidden fruit. God is not the author of *death,* but of *life!*

Forasmuch then as the children are partakers of flesh and blood, he also himself (Jesus) likewise took part of the same; that through death he might destroy him that had the power of death, that is, the devil.

Hebrews 2:14

Death is of the Devil; it's an enemy of God and of man. Sin caused Adam to die. Sin brought death. *For the wages of sin is death; but the gift of God is eternal life* (Rom. 6:23).

The Body Was Designed To Recreate Itself

Adam's body was designed to live forever. Medical science can't tell why people die. They know some die from sickness and disease, but they don't know why the body ages. It was designed to recreate itself every seven to eleven years. There isn't one cell in your body today that was there eleven years ago.

The day Adam ate of the tree which God said would produce death, he became mortal. He chose mortality in the Garden.

And the Lord God took the man, and put him into the garden of Eden to dress it and to keep it.

Genesis 2:15

Adam had all authority to subdue and have dominion over every creeping thing on earth. God put him in the Garden to keep it. The Hebrew word *keep* means "to hedge it about, guard, and protect." In other words, "to preserve it from all intruders."

And the Lord God commanded the man, saying, Of every tree of the garden thou mayest freely eat: but of the tree of the knowledge of good and evil, thou shalt not eat of it: for in the day that thou eatest thereof thou shalt surely die.

Genesis 2:16,17

Adam did die. He died spiritually the instant he sinned. He didn't know how to die physically because his body was designed to live forever. It took Satan over 900 years to teach him how to die.

But of the tree of the knowledge of good and evil, thou shalt not eat (v. 17).

God didn't want Adam to eat of the tree of knowledge which was really knowing the difference between good and evil. The Hebrew says, "the knowledge of blessing and calamity."

The fall of man was directly connected to his tongue. *Adam gained knowledge of how to produce blessing and calamity by the words of his mouth.* The word *evil* used here means "adversity, affliction, bad, calamity, grief, hurt, harm, and trouble." Adam ate of that fruit. That was dumb!

God had told him, "Don't do it. If you do, you are going to die. You will become a spiritually dead man. Yes, you are going to gain knowledge—*the knowledge of calamity!*" Because Adam already knew how to speak blessings, he only gained the knowledge of calamity and *how to produce it.*

The serpent was more subtil than any beast of the field which the Lord God had made (Gen. 3:1). God created the earth and put man on it. Satan came on the scene in the form of a serpent. He had to enter a body so he could be manifested on earth. He had to come through some form of creation to reach Adam, so he used the body of a serpent.

Satan can't come directly to your spirit; he has to approach your body—*and you can shut him off with your will!* Your mind was given to you as a door to keep your heart (spirit). *You are the keeper of that door* and you can shut it anytime.

And the serpent said unto the woman, Ye shall not surely die: for God doth know that in the day ye eat thereof, then your eyes shall be opened, and ye shall be as gods, knowing good and evil.

Genesis 3:4,5

Notice that Satan said, "You'll be as gods." There is the great deception. Was all that Satan said a lie? No. It was a half-truth. *Elohim* is the Hebrew word used for *gods.* Adam and Eve were so excited over Satan saying, "You will become as *Elohim* (gods)," that they didn't pay attention to the other part—knowing calamity.

Adam Had No Need For Intellectual Knowledge

If all Adam and Eve were to gain was evil, Adam would have turned it down.

Until he gave his authority to Satan, Adam was operating in revelation knowledge. Satan offered him an alternative to the tree of life. The tree of calamity would give the *ability* to produce calamity. The tree of life contained *everything* Adam needed. He could eat freely of it. It would produce the knowledge of how to get everything good—*by the words of his mouth.*

A wholesome tongue is a tree of life: but perverseness therein is a breach in the spirit.
Proverbs 15:4

The mouth of a righteous man is a well of life.

Proverbs 10:11

The fruit of the righteous is a tree of life.
Proverbs 11:30

Happy is the man that findeth wisdom, and the man that getteth understanding. For the merchandise of it is better than the merchandise of silver, and the gain thereof than fine gold.

She is more precious than rubies: and all the things thou canst desire are not to be compared unto her. Length of days is in her right hand; and in her left hand riches and honour.

*Her ways are ways of pleasantness, and all her paths are peace. She is a **tree of life** to them that lay hold upon her.*

Proverbs 3:13-18

Hope deferred maketh the heart sick: but when the desire cometh, it (desire) *is a **tree of life**.*

Proverbs 13:12

Fruit of the Lips

Adam had access to the tree of life which would give him wisdom, a wholesome tongue, righteous fruit from his lips, and desire. (Desire makes one speak in order to bring forth fruit of the lips.)

How prophetic are the words of Proverbs 13:2,3. *A man shall eat good by the fruit of his mouth: but the soul of the transgressors shall eat violence. He that keepeth his mouth keepeth his life.*

Adam ate of the transgressor's (forbidden) fruit. He ate of violence (calamity), lost his spiritual life, and eventually lost his physical life. He gained knowledge of how to produce calamity *by the words of his mouth.* When he bowed his knee to Satan, *he lost control of the good.* **Adam lost the ability to control his tongue.**

The third chapter of James tells us *the tongue is an unruly evil, full of deadly poison, and is set on fire of hell.* Adam's tongue was set on fire of hell when he ate the fruit. It poisoned his tongue, and he lost the ability to control it.

How was Adam to control and subdue the earth? By *the words of his mouth,* using his faith—by *speaking things into existence.*

Adam was created a full-grown man with no need for intellectual knowledge. He was already operating in revelation knowledge. He was subordinate only to God. God's Spirit was in contact with Adam's spirit.

And when the woman saw that the tree was good for food, and that it was pleasant to the eyes, and a tree to be desired to make one wise, she took of the fruit thereof, and did eat, and gave also unto her husband with her; and he did eat.

Genesis 3:6

Some of you thought Adam was off somewhere in the back of the Garden picking fruit or naming bugs when Eve got into trouble! But that's not the way it happened. Adam was standing right there with her. In fact, Adam sinned *first*.

God told Adam to subdue the earth and have dominion over every living thing. (Gen. 1:28.) Wasn't that snake a living creature?

God said, "You have dominion over him; subdue him. Guard the Garden; hedge it about. *Protect it from all intruders*." That was a command, not just a suggestion.

Adam was standing right there, listening to every word the serpent said, and he deliberately disobeyed God. He could have said, "Serpent, in the name of Almighty God, I demand that you leave this planet and never return." In an instant of time Satan would have been banished from the earth.

But Adam didn't do that. *He deliberately disobeyed God*. The Bible states that Eve was deceived, but Adam was not. (1 Tim. 2:14.) Eve was deceived because Adam didn't do what God had told him to do. If he had obeyed God and used his authority, Eve would not have been deceived.

Adam stood there with all the authority vested in him from God the Father to protect the Garden and all that it contained, but he didn't use his authority. He bowed his knee to an outlaw spirit and allowed the curse to come. He invited death and destruction.

Disobedience—Deception

The first thing that happened was disobedience, then deception. It was Adam's *disobedience* that caused Eve to be deceived.

We find in Genesis 3:14-19 that a curse came because of the disobedience. In verse 22 we read, *And the Lord God said, Behold, the man is become as one of us . . . .* And Adam was driven from the Garden. (v. 24.)

You can see that Satan had told them a half-truth. God said, "Man has become as one of us to know good and evil." Adam had gained the knowledge of how to produce both blessing and calamity by the words of his mouth. He was created to operate on the same level of faith with God, then he gained the knowledge of how to set it in motion.

But in gaining that knowledge, he disobeyed God and bowed his knee to Satan. He lost control of his tongue and had trouble using it for good.

James said of the tongue that it is *set on fire of hell . . . an unruly evil, full of deadly poison* (James 3:6,8).

God said, *Man is become as one of us to know good and evil: and now, lest he put forth his hand, and take also of the tree of life, and eat, and live for ever* (Gen. 3:22). Notice that the sentence stopped there. God quit talking and put Adam out of the Garden.

Therefore the Lord God sent him forth from the garden of Eden, to till the ground from whence he was taken. So he drove out the man; and he placed at the east of the garden of Eden Cherubims, and a flaming sword which turned every way, to keep the way of the tree of life (vv. 23,24).

Adam could have eaten of the tree of life and established immortality, but instead *he ate of the forbidden tree and became mortal.* So God said, "Get him out of the Garden because if he gets hold of that tree of life, he will live forever in that sinful state."

You can see the wisdom and mercy of God in that. What would have happened if Adam had partaken of the tree of life after he had sinned? The curse was already there; so when sickness, disease, and the other horrible afflictions began to control man's life, he would have lived throughout eternity with no hope of ever being delivered from the curse. There would have been no hope of deliverance from all the horrible pains caused by the diabolic and devilish diseases Satan had brought about through the curse.

Because Adam bowed his knee to Satan, he set in motion the curses: sickness, disease, calamity, and disaster. If man had eaten of the tree of life after he had sinned, he would have lived forever in that sinful state. Every evil person, every criminal who ever lived on earth, would still be alive today! It would have produced hell on earth!

God created man with a will. Man was free to choose. He had the choice of immortality or mortality, and he chose to become mortal. It was Adam's choice. The wages of sin is death. Without sin, there would be no death.

God Drove Adam Out For Man's Own Good

God put Adam out of the Garden after he had sinned to keep him from tapping the tree of life. Otherwise, he would have lived forever in that sinful state. Ezekiel 18:4 says, *The soul that sinneth, it shall die.*

Someone said that Adam couldn't have lived forever after he sinned, because if he had, God would have lied. No, there are two deaths. Adam died *spiritually* the instant he ate of the tree of knowledge. But if he had eaten of the tree of life after sinning, he would never have died *physically*. He would have been a spiritually dead man throughout eternity with no way to rid himself of the sickness and disease that came by the curse. Man would have been in hell on earth!

Satan Was After the Tree of Life

There was a reason for God driving Adam and Eve out of the Garden. He

wanted to get them away from the tree
of life. Satan had his eye on that tree
and wanted to get his hands on it. He
had no authority on earth until he
tapped into man's power and authority.
(Adam had given his own God-given
authority over to Satan.)

Someone might ask, "Why didn't
Satan just go over and pick the fruit and
eat it?"

He couldn't do that. Satan is a spirit
being, and spirits have no authority in
earth without a body. If they did, evil
spirits would tear the earth to pieces,
destroying it in a moment of time. But
they can't do that. They must enter into
a body to destroy.

Man's body gives him authority on
earth. Satan tapped into man's
authority by using the body of the
serpent. He tempted Eve through the
serpent and caused Adam to commit
high treason. The only way Satan could
get to the tree of life was to get Adam to
sin and become subordinate to him, for
Adam was the god of this world.

After Adam became subordinate to
Satan, Satan became his lord. Whatever
Adam could tap into naturally, Satan

could have. Satan was trying to get Adam to tap into the tree of life. If he had done so, Satan would have partaken of it also!

But God is smarter than that! He put Adam out of the Garden to stop that from coming to pass!

Curse Upon the Serpent

And the Lord God said unto the serpent, Because thou hast done this, thou art cursed above all cattle, and above every beast of the field; upon thy belly shalt thou go, and dust shalt thou eat all the days of thy life.

Genesis 3:14

Evidently, the serpent didn't crawl on his belly until the curse. But because he allowed himself to be used by that evil spirit, Satan, the serpent was cursed.

A Prophecy Fulfilled by Jesus

And I will put enmity between thee and the woman, and between thy seed and her seed . . . (v. 15).

Notice He didn't say, "the seed of the man," but, "the seed of the woman." Jesus became the seed of woman. He was born of a woman; He had no earthly father.

God says here, . . . *it shall bruise thy head, and thou shalt bruise his heel* (v. 15). In other words, Satan will only be able to affect the feet, but Jesus will crush Satan's head.

Woman's Part of the Curse

Unto the woman he said, I will greatly multiply thy sorrow and thy conception; in sorrow thou shalt bring forth children; and thy desire shall be to thy husband, and he shall rule over thee (v. 16).

Some people think that part of the curse was that women would have to bear children, but God had already told Adam and Eve to multiply and replenish the earth. The curse was that there would be *sorrow in conception*.

Adam's Part

And unto Adam he said, Because thou hast hearkened unto the voice of thy wife, and hast eaten of the tree, of which I commanded thee, saying, Thou shalt not eat of it: cursed is the ground for thy sake; in sorrow shalt thou eat of it all the days of thy

*life; thorns also and thistles shall it bring
forth to thee; and thou shalt eat the herb of
the field* (vv. 17,18).

Thorns and thistles are part of the
curse. Those that crucified Jesus made a
crown of thorns and put it on His head.
The thorns are symbols of the full curse
Jesus had to bear for us.

*And Adam called his wife's name Eve;
because she was the mother of all living*
(v. 20). Here is something you possibly
had not seen: God did not name Eve.
Adam named his wife, "Eve."

We read in Genesis 5:2, *Male and
female created he them; and blessed them,
and called their name Adam, in the day
when they were created.* God called them
both "Adam" when He created them.

Satan tried to tap into the tree of life
and failed. God put Adam out of that
Garden after he handed his authority
over to Satan. Satan could not get at the
tree of life. God had other plans.

The story is told of a little boy in
Sunday school who heard the teacher
tell them to draw a picture of something
they had learned in class that day. The
boy drew a picture of a red Cadillac
convertible with an old gray-haired man

in the front seat and a young couple in the back seat.

The teacher looked at the picture and said, "Jimmy, we didn't study anything like that today."

"Yes, we did," said Jimmy. "Don't you remember? That's God, driving Adam and Eve out of the Garden!"

5
Noah's Covenant

As you look in Genesis, chapter 6, you will see that God made a covenant with man after Adam committed high treason. God had given Adam dominion over the earth. He had rulership—authority and dominion—but he turned it over to Satan.

Before the Fall, God came to walk and talk with Adam in the Garden. They had an intimate fellowship. Adam had revelation knowledge that flowed from God, the Father. But when Adam bowed his knee to Satan, he shut God out. God found Himself on the outside looking in. His man, Adam, had lost his authority.

Satan had come in illegally and was lording it over the earth. He had become the god of the world system, and the world was becoming desperately wicked.

God Establishes a Covenant

God needed a legal way to get back into the affairs of earth, so He made a covenant with Noah. *But with thee will I establish my covenant; and thou shalt come into the ark, thou, and thy sons, and thy wife, and thy sons' wives with thee* (Gen. 6:18).

You may ask, "Why did God have to make a covenant with Noah?"

Noah had a body, and it gave him a certain amount of authority on earth. God had limited Himself in what He could do because of what He had said and done in Genesis 1:26-28.

Now don't get the idea that God doesn't have power to do what He wants to do. He has the power; but because of His Word, He can't do some things. God couldn't come to earth and say, "Adam, I'm going to wipe out you and Satan. I'm going to get that authority back. I'm going to do this whole thing over and make another man out of the dust of the earth." He couldn't do that because the dust of the earth didn't belong to Him. His man, Adam, had given it to Satan.

Satan had gained ascendancy in the earth by gaining Adam's authority, and God was left on the outside. God couldn't come here in His divine power and wipe them out. He had to move in an area where it would be ruled legal by the Supreme Court of the Universe. Adam was the one with authority until he sinned; then he became subordinate to Satan.

God gained entrance back into the earth through the covenant He made with Noah. He was still limited in what He could do because of His Word. He started putting things into motion through the covenant.

Covenant with Man, Beast, and Earth

And God spake unto Noah, and to his sons with him, saying, And I, behold, I establish my covenant with you, and with your seed after you; and with every living creature that is with you, of the fowl, of the cattle, and of every beast of the earth with you; from all that go out of the ark, to every beast of the earth.

And I will establish my covenant with you; neither shall all flesh be cut off any more by the waters of a flood; neither shall there any more be a flood to destroy the earth.

And God said, This is the token of the covenant which I make between me and you and every living creature that is with you, for perpetual generations.

Genesis 9:8-12

God put a rainbow in the sky as a token of the covenant He made with Noah. (v. 13.) He said, "It will not happen anymore. I'll even make a covenant with the animals you take out of the ark, and they will be perpetual generations."

God made a covenant and established it in the earth. You see God moving again to set things back in order. He made a covenant with a man, and *mankind still had some authority by choice.* Man was still able to operate here. He still had a choice even though he had become spiritually dead.

A Sin Covering

God established a way wherein He could cover man's sins by shedding blood and offering sacrifices. This only covered sins. It didn't actually redeem man.

The first thing Noah did when he came out of the ark after the Flood was to build an altar and plant a vineyard. The next thing mentioned is that Noah got rip-roaring drunk. (Gen. 9:20,21.)

By this, you can see there was still an evil hold on the earth. Satan was still at work after the Flood. Generation after generation, man degenerated from the righteous state in which God had created him.

And the whole earth was of one language, and of one speech . . . And they said, Go to, let us build us a city and a tower, whose top may reach unto heaven; and let us make us a name, lest we be scattered abroad upon the face of the whole earth. And the Lord came down to see the city and the tower, which the children of men builded (Gen. 11:1,4,5).

Notice, they were not going to build a tower in order to get to God's throne! They said, "We are going to make a name for ourselves." They were after a name.

Then God said something awesome about man whom He had created. *Behold, the people is one, and they have all one language; and this they begin to do: and now nothing will be restrained from them, which they have imagined to do* (v. 6).

God was saying that there was *nothing* the people could not do because they were one in speech and unity. Those people were devil worshipers. They had gone away from God.

God said of the man He had created, even after the man had degenerated to such a low estate, "Anything man can imagine or conceive in his heart, he can perform!"

God confounded their language. They were scattered abroad upon the earth, and it stopped them temporarily. But they had already imagined they could do it, and it continued to grow in the imaginations of men.

Science picked it up in our generation, and we saw it come to pass! We sat in our living rooms, in July of 1969, and saw the words God had spoken come to pass: "Nothing shall restrain them." Man had landed on the moon! He had imagined it. He had meditated on it. He had dwelt on it. Then it came to pass. He stepped out of his spaceship and stuck an American flag in the dust.

God said man could do it! He said, "Anything man can imagine, he can bring to pass!" God said, "Nothing will restrain man, not even confounding his language." It slowed him down temporarily, but it didn't stop him.

You see a different story emerging from the creation of man. This is quite different from most of our religious ideas. Man was *not* created to be a little worm in the dust! He is capable of operating on the same level of faith with God.

Science tells us that man is not using even one tenth of his capabilities—just a minute part. Why? Because man is inhibited by forces of the evil one. But when man was redeemed and born again, he became a *new creation!*

The Apostle Paul said, *If any man be in Christ, he is a new creation: old things are passed away; behold, all things are become new* (2 Cor. 5:17).

Satan can't handle the new creation! Thank God!

6
Abraham's Covenant

God made a promise to Abram: "I'll bless those that bless you." America is blessed today because we have blessed Israel. Any nation that comes against Israel will be cursed.

Now the Lord had said unto Abram, Get thee out of thy country, and from thy kindred, and from thy father's house, unto a land that I will shew thee: And I will make of thee a great nation, and I will bless thee, and make thy name great; and thou shalt be a blessing: And I will bless them that bless thee, and curse him that curseth thee: and in thee shall all families of the earth be blessed (Gen. 12:1-3).

In Genesis 14 is a story of several kings who came against the kings of Sodom and Gomorrah, overthrew them, and took Lot (Abram's nephew) and his family, with all of their goods.

One person escaped and told Abram what had happened. Abram gathered the people of his household together and went after the five kings. He had sufficient battalion to recapture all that had been taken and win the battle against the kings.

And the king of Sodom said unto Abram, Give me the persons, and take the goods to thyself. And Abram said to the king of Sodom, I have lift up mine hand unto the Lord, the most high God, the possessor of heaven and earth, that I will not take from a thread even to a shoelatchet, and that I will not take any thing that is thine, lest thou shouldest say, I have made Abram rich (Gen. 14:21-23).

Abram made the commitment to God, "I won't even take the shoelatchet out of that man's shoes, lest he would say he has made me rich."

In chapter 15, verses 1-18, God talked to Abram again. *In the same day the Lord made a covenant with Abram . . .* (v. 18).

Then in Genesis 17:1-5:

And when Abram was ninety years old and nine, the Lord appeared to Abram, and said unto him, I am the Almighty God; walk before me, and be thou perfect. And I will

*make my covenant between me and thee, and
will multiply thee exceedingly.*

*And Abram fell on his face: and God
talked with him, saying, As for me, behold,
my covenant is with thee, and thou shalt be
a father of many nations. Neither shall thy
name any more be called Abram, but thy
name shall be Abraham; for a father of many
nations have I made thee.*

God established a blood covenant
with Abram in chapter 15. Blood
covenants are established in every
nation in the world today, even in the
most remote parts of the earth. Blood
covenants originally came from God. A
blood covenant is the strongest
covenant going.

If someone makes a blood covenant
with you, it literally means that what
they have is yours and what you have is
theirs—even to your life if the other one
has need of it.

This is what God said to Abraham:
*As for me, behold, my covenant is with thee,
and thou shalt be a father of many nations.
Neither shall thy name any more be called
Abram, but thy name shall be Abraham; for
a father of many nations have I made thee*
(vv. 4,5). The name *Abraham* means

"father of a great multitude." God is saying, "I've already done it. I've already made you a father of many nations."

And I will establish my covenant between me and thee and thy seed after thee in their generations for an everlasting covenant, to be a God unto thee, and to thy seed after thee (v. 7).

Notice God said, "I've established My Covenant between Me and thee." In other words, "The Covenant is standing between Me and you. If anyone gets to Me or to you, they're going to have to deal with this Covenant. If I'm going to get to you, Abraham, I will have to come through this Covenant. If you want to get to Me, you will have to come through this Covenant. In other words, the Covenant will regulate how I deal with you and how you deal with Me."

In this, God is establishing some legal entry into the earth, and He is giving Abraham access to Himself. Through that Covenant Abraham can draw help from God, draw wisdom from God, and draw an anointing from

God in the earth so that the Devil's works can be destroyed.

God told Abraham to circumcise himself. This was a seal of the righteousness of the faith which he had. (Rom. 4:11.) This Covenant gave God legal entry into the earth through Abraham. Each covenant God made became stronger.

Until that time God was, to a certain extent, still on the outside looking in. He needed a legal entry through man so that He could destroy the works of the Devil who was running rampant on earth.

And the Lord appeared unto him in the plains of Mamre: and he sat in the tent door in the heat of the day; and he lift up his eyes and looked, and, lo, three men stood by him: and when he saw them, he ran to meet them from the tent door, and bowed himself toward the ground (Gen. 18:1,2).

Two of these men were angels; one, evidently, was God Himself. Abraham was God's avenue of entry into the earth. God had come to talk about Sodom and Gomorrah with Abraham.

And the men rose up from thence, and looked toward Sodom: and Abraham went

*with them to bring them on the way. And
the Lord said, Shall I hide from Abraham
that thing which I do; seeing that Abraham
shall surely become a great and mighty
nation, and all the nations of the earth shall
be blessed in him?* (Gen. 18:16,18).

Abraham's nephew Lot was in
Sodom, a city that had become exceedingly sinful and wicked. God wanted to
destroy Sodom and Gomorrah, but He
talked it over with Abraham since He
had made a Covenant with him.

*And the Lord said, Because the cry of
Sodom and Gomorrah is great, and because
their sin is very grievous; I will go down
now, and see whether they have done
altogether according to the cry of it, which is
come unto me; and if not, I will know. And
the men turned their faces from thence, and
went toward Sodom: but Abraham stood yet
before the Lord* (vv. 20-22).

Abraham knew Lot was in the city.
*And Abraham drew near, and said, Wilt
thou also destroy the righteous with the
wicked? Peradventure there be fifty
righteous within the city: wilt thou also
destroy and not spare the place for the fifty
righteous that are therein? That be far from
thee to do after this manner, to slay the*

righteous with the wicked: and that the righteous should be as the wicked, that be far from thee: Shall not the Judge of all the earth do right? (vv. 23-25).

God said, "No, I wouldn't destroy it if I found fifty righteous." (v. 26.)

Abraham was subordinate to God, but God was counseling with Abraham. He started with fifty righteous persons then came down to ten.

And he (Abraham) *said, Oh let not the Lord be angry, and I will speak yet but this once: Peradventure ten shall be found there. And he said, I will not destroy it for ten's sake. And the Lord went his way, as soon as he had left communing with Abraham: and Abraham returned unto his place* (vv 32,33).

God would not destroy the righteous with the wicked.

And there came two angels to Sodom at even; and Lot sat in the gate of Sodom: and Lot seeing them rose up to meet them; and he bowed himself with his face toward the ground; and he said, Behold now, my lords turn in, I pray you . . . (Gen. 19:1,2).

God sent the angels there to check things out. They knew the purpose of the mission. Lot immediately recognized them as angels. He took them into his house and said, . . . *tarry all night, and wash your feet, and ye shall rise up early, and go on your ways. And they said, Nay; but we will abide in the street all night* (v. 2).

Lot Finds Favor

And it came to pass, when they had brought them forth abroad, that he said, Escape for thy life; look not behind thee, neither stay thou in all the plain; escape to the mountain, lest thou be consumed.

And Lot said unto them, Oh, not so my Lord: Behold now, thy servant hath found grace in thy sight, and thou hast magnified thy mercy, which thou hast shewed unto me in saving my life; and I cannot escape to the mountain, lest some evil take me, and I die:

Behold now, this city is near to flee unto, and it is a little one: Oh, let me escape thither (is it not a little one?) and my soul shall live.

And he said unto him, See, I have accepted thee concerning this thing also, that I will not overthrow this city, for the which thou hast spoken (vv. 17-21).

A righteous man had power with God and the angels. Lot wanted to go to another city. He didn't want to spend the night in the mountains. We find later that Lot did leave the city and go into the mountains to dwell there. But he didn't want to go that night. He said, "It's just a little city. Don't destroy it." His request was granted because he asked.

You see, **authority still lies with righteous men!**

Haste thee, escape thither; for I cannot do any thing, till thou be come thither. Therefore the name of the city was called Zoar (v. 22).

The angel said, "I can't do anything until you get out of here." Why? Because God had made a Covenant with Abraham.

Abraham said, *That be far from thee . . . to slay the righteous with the wicked . . . Shall not the Judge of all the earth do right?* (Gen. 18:25). You can see the authority of the righteousness which is by faith. *Abraham believed God, and it was accounted to him for righteousness* (Gal. 3:6).

The Covenant Proven

The Blood Covenant meant that what was God's was Abraham's and what was Abraham's was God's—even to their lives, if necessary, with no questions asked.

This Covenant was of great benefit to Abraham and God. It was so strong that God swore by Himself to perform it. If either God or Abraham broke the Covenant, it meant death.

This Covenant was so strong that God had to prove it to be valid. He had to prove that Abraham was capable of performing his part. God knew Satan would challenge it if it were not proven before the whole universe. Certainly God was able and willing to perform His part, but all the universe had to know that Abraham could and would perform his part. *If Abraham failed, the Covenant would be void.*

The promised son, Isaac, had been born to Abraham and Sarah. Abraham was receiving the benefits of the Covenant, and everything was going great. Then we find a strange request from God.

*And it came to pass after these things
that God did tempt (prove) Abraham, and
said unto him, Abraham: and he said
Behold, here I am.*

*And he said, Take now thy son, thine
only son Isaac, whom thou lovest, and get
thee into the land of Moriah; and offer him
there for a burnt offering upon one of the
mountains which I will tell thee of.*

*And Abraham rose up early in the
morning, and saddled his ass, and took two
of his young men with him, and Isaac his
son, and clave the wood for the burnt
offering, and rose up, and went unto the
place of which God had told him.*

Genesis 22:1-3

As you read this, you can't help but
think how Abraham must have felt as
they made their way up the mountain
He had the wood, the fire, the knife
then Isaac asked, "Where is the lamb
for the burnt offering?" (v. 7.)

Abraham spoke one of the most
prophetic statements ever made when
he answered Isaac. *My son, God will
provide himself a lamb for a burnt offering*
(v. 8). That was exactly what God was
about to do: *provide Himself—God
manifested in the flesh, Jesus—to be the*

sacrifice forever! In obedience, Abraham bound his son and laid him on the altar.

And Abraham stretched forth his hand, and took the knife to slay his son.

And the angel of the Lord called unto him out of heaven, and said, Abraham, Abraham: and he said, Here am I. And he said, Lay not thine hand upon the lad, neither do thou any thing unto him: for now I know that thou fearest God, seeing thou hast not withheld thy son, thine only son from me.

And Abraham lifted up his eyes, and looked, and behold behind him a ram caught in a thicket by his horns: and Abraham went and took the ram, and offered him up for a burnt offering in the stead of his son (vv. 10-13).

Evidently, Abraham knew something of what the Blood Covenant required of him for he was obedient to what seemed an unreasonable request. Not once did he hesitate in offering his only son.

Oh, how these immortal words ring out! **Abraham believed God, and it was accounted to him for righteousness.**

Notice in Romans 4:11, *And he received the sign of circumcision, a seal of the righteousness of the faith which he had yet being uncircumcised: that he might be the father of all them that believe.*

First Corinthians 1:30 caps it off by telling us Jesus *is made unto us wisdom, and righteousness, and sanctification, and redemption.* Abraham's obedience accomplished more for us than it did for him!

*And the angel of the Lord called unto Abraham out of heaven the second time, and said, By myself have I sworn, saith the Lord, for because thou **hast done** this thing, and hast not withheld thy son, thine only son . . .* (Gen. 22:15,16).

God was saying to Abraham, "You have already done it." Because Abraham was willing to raise the knife against his child, God said to him, "It is received as done."

What was behind Abraham's obedience to what seemed a most unreasonable request? God Himself commanded, *Thou shalt not kill* (Ex. 20:13); but He told Abraham to offer his only son as a sacrifice. In the natural that just doesn't make sense.

This thing is so far-reaching that few people understand it. But a blood covenant had been made, and a covenant is a contract which binds *both* parties. God made it with an earthly man.

God knew that Satan was going to challenge what He was about to do, for God was going to bring eternal redemption to man.

Before we go any farther with this subject, I'd like to share an example with you that the Lord shared with me. It will help you understand why God made such a request of Abraham.

Let's say that your city is accepting bids on a ten-million-dollar building at ten o'clock Monday morning. A man who has been sleeping in a box car for several days reads in the local paper about the bid letting and says, "I used to build houses. I believe I'll bid on this job!"

But instead of bidding the ten million dollars, he turns in a bid of two million. For sure, he's the low bidder! But before the bid is qualified, he must prove he can perform his part of the contract. They will find that he slept in a box car, that he's not bonded, that he has no credit and can't supply materials. In short, he can't perform what he agreed to do. A contract with him is a worthless document. It couldn't be binding because the man doesn't have the ability to perform the contract—to carry out his obligation.

God knew Satan was going to challenge him about the legality of making such a Covenant with a man on earth. Satan was going to say, "Man is not capable of fulfilling that contract; it's a one-sided deal. It's invalid. Abraham won't go through with it. He won't give his life."

God, in His wisdom, proved Abraham to be capable and willing. What did God have in his mind when He said to Abraham, "Go offer your son"? Abraham prophesied about God's sacrifice when he said to Isaac, *My son, God will provide himself a lamb for a burnt offering.*

God was setting the stage for the greatest manifestation of love the world had ever known. God was saying, "I'm going to prove the Covenant I made with Abraham is legal. I'm going to prove, once and for all, that Abraham will keep My Covenant."

So, He demanded that Abraham sacrifice his only son. God didn't ask Abraham for his own life; He asked for his *only son* (the one God said would be heir to all, and through him would His Seed be. Actually, the *Seed* God is talking about is Jesus.) God said, ''I have sworn by Myself because you have done this thing.''

Abraham performed his part very well. God called it *done;* and in the Supreme Court of the Universe, it is written as done: that Abraham gave his son. (Heb. 11:17-19.) It was a legal document that actually stands as a witness to Satan and all the demons of hell that Abraham *gave his son!*

God has proven that document to be legal. The Blood Covenant God made with Abraham was *valid* and *will stand forever!*

Now—*God could give His Son for the world!* Abraham's obedience in offering his son made it possible for God to offer His Son, Jesus, as the Eternal Sacrifice for *eternal redemption.*

The far-reaching effects of what could have happened staggers the imagination. What if Abraham had not validated that Covenant? What if he had said, "I will give anything *except* my only son"?

If Abraham had not given Isaac, God could not have given Jesus! The Covenant would have been void. It would have been illegal for God *to provide Himself a Lamb*.

Abraham's obedience to the Covenant gave God the legal entry into the earth to redeem man with His Son, Jesus.

7
The Miraculous Conception

We find that God and man are working *together* in order to destroy the kingdom of darkness. Man's earthly authority is needed to go along with God's ability to perform the work. All of the universe must have sighed in relief the day Abraham raised the knife against Isaac. The redemption of all mankind rested upon his obedience, and God swore an oath that shall be forever.

By myself have I sworn, saith the Lord, for because thou hast done this thing, and hast not withheld thy son, thine only son: that in blessing I will bless thee, and in multiplying I will multiply thy seed as the stars of the heaven, and as the sand which is upon the sea shore; and thy seed shall possess the gate of his enemies (Gen. 22:16,17).

You ought to underline in your Bible: *Thy seed shall possess the gate of his enemies.* Not *seeds,* but *Seed,* as one. He is talking about Jesus. *Jesus is the Seed!*

If you are born of God, you are the seed of Abraham!

Let's notice a passage in Genesis 24:60. *And they blessed Rebekah, and said unto her, Thou art our sister, be thou the mother of thousands of millions, and let thy seed possess the gate of those which hate them.* In those days if you possessed the gate of any city, that city was under your control. This is what God was saying.

With that in mind, let's look at Isaiah 7:14. *Therefore the Lord himself shall give you a sign; Behold, a virgin shall conceive, and bear a son, and shall call his name Immanuel.*

Remember when God was telling of the curse? He said to the serpent, "The seed of woman shall bruise your head." (Gen. 3:15.)

Then the prophecy came forth out of Isaiah: *Behold, a virgin shall conceive, and bear a son . . . .* It could not be the seed of man, but the seed of a *woman.* Why did God say this through His prophet? Why didn't God just do it? You will find, as you study your Bible, that *God*

never did anything without saying it first.
This was hundreds of years before the
prophecy came to pass. This is the way
God's faith works!

God framed the worlds with *words.*
He was framing this and setting it in
motion by saying it through His prophet: *A virgin shall conceive and bear a son.*

The Bible tells us that it is impossible
for God to lie. Why? Because He
releases sufficient faith in every word
He speaks to bring it to pass. *There is
faith in every word of God!*

Mary Received the Word

*Therefore the Lord himself shall give you
a sign; Behold, a virgin shall conceive, and
bear a son, and shall call his name Immanuel*
(God with us).

The Word became flesh. *In the
beginning was the Word, and the Word was
with God, and the Word was God.* God
spoke it through His prophet Isaiah 750
years before it came to pass.

In the first chapter of Luke, God sent
an angel to talk to Zacharias about his
wife Elisabeth conceiving and bearing a
child. In verse 18, Zacharias said unto
the angel, *Whereby shall I know this? for I*

am an old man, and my wife well stricken in years.

The angel answered and said unto him, "I am Gabriel, who stands in the presence of God, and you should not have said that!" (v. 19.)

Zacharias wanted a sign that it was going to happen. That's just like earth people! We'll believe the postman or the guy at the gas station; but if God says something, we say, "Show me a sign!"

God, in His wisdom, knew He had to get Zacharias' mouth shut or he would blow the whole deal. When God dealt with Abraham, He just renamed him so that every time someone called his name, it built his faith. (*Abraham* means "father of many nations.") But what about Zacharias? God had to shut his mouth.

And, behold, thou shalt be dumb, and not able to speak, until the day that these things shall be performed, because thou believest not my words, which shall be fulfilled in their season (v. 20).

When it was fulfilled, Zacharias got his voice back. Some of us would be

better off if we lost our voices until the
deals we're involved with are over!

*And in the sixth month the same angel
Gabriel was sent from God unto a city of
Galilee, named Nazareth, to a virgin
espoused to a man whose name was Joseph,
of the house of David; and the virgin's name
was Mary.*

*And the angel came in unto her, and
said, Hail, thou that art highly favoured,
the Lord is with thee: blessed art thou
among women. And when she saw him, she
was troubled at his saying, and cast in her
mind what manner of salutation this should
be.*

*And the angel said unto her, Fear not,
Mary: for thou hast found favour with God.
And, behold, thou shalt conceive in thy
womb, and bring forth a son, and shalt call
his name JESUS.*

Luke 1:26-31

The word *behold* means "look."
Look at what? Look at the picture I'm
going to paint with words: *Behold, thou
shalt conceive in thy womb.*

The woman has no seed. The male
carries the seed. . . . *Thou shalt conceive
in thy womb . . . He shall be great and shall
be called the Son of the Highest: and the*

*Lord God shall give unto him the throne of
his father David: and he shall reign over the
house of Jacob for ever; and of his kingdom
there shall be no end. Then said Mary unto
the angel, How shall this be, seeing I know
not a man?* (Luke 1:31-34).

Mary didn't doubt that it was going
to happen. She just wanted to know
how.

*And the angel answered and said unto
her, The Holy Ghost shall come upon thee*
(v. 35). The Greek states "as a cloud,"
or the Presence of God.

Remember, John 1:1 says, *In the
beginning was the Word, and the Word was
with God, and the Word was God.* Verse 14
says, *And the Word was made flesh.* The
Word was made flesh—the *Word!*

There are people today who say it
couldn't possibly have happened. They
try to go at it strictly biologically, when
it was both spiritual and biological. It
was the Word which was conceived in
her womb.

**It was an act of the God-kind of
faith that caused the miraculous
conception.**

*The Holy Ghost shall come upon thee,
and the power of the Highest shall over-*

*shadow thee: therefore also that holy thing
which shall be born of thee shall be called the
Son of God. And, behold, thy cousin
Elisabeth, she hath also conceived a son in
her old age: and this is the sixth month with
her, who was called barren. For with God
nothing shall be impossible* (Luke 1:35-37).

The literal Greek states: "It is
possible for God to perform His every
declaration."

*And Mary said, Behold the handmaid of
the Lord; be it unto me according to thy
word* (v. 38).

Jesus tells us how the God-kind of
faith works in Mark 11:23. *Whosoever
shall say . . . and shall not doubt in his
heart, but shall believe that those things
which he saith shall come to pass; he shall
have whatsoever he saith.*

God found a woman who said,
"Behold (look), You have found her.
You have found the one. *Be it done unto
me according to thy word.*" According to
feelings? No. *According to thy word. The
Word was God, and Jesus was the Word
made flesh.*

It was the Word that was made
flesh. Mary conceived the Word of God
in her heart; then she went to

Elisabeth's house and told her, "He
hath done great things." (Luke 1:49.)
How did she know? Because the angel
of the Lord had told her, and she
received that Word.

Do you think she felt any different?
No. Do you think she looked any
different? No. What was her evidence?
Faith and her words! "He hath done
great things." The Word said she was
filled with the Holy Ghost, and she
began to prophesy. She had conceived
the Word of God in her spirit.

Here is what the Spirit of God said
to me about that situation: "Mary conceived the Word sent to her by the angel
(God's Word) and conceived it in the
womb of her spirit. Once it was conceived in her spirit, it manifested itself
in her physical body. *She received and
conceived the Word of God in her spirit.*"

If she had said, "Forget it, it won't
work," God would have had to find
another woman. But notice Mary's
words, "He hath done great things."

She accepted God's Word. She
believed God's Word.

Theologians say *it couldn't possibly
have happened* because they want to

place it in the biological realm. The Bible didn't say she conceived in any other way. It said, *The Word was made flesh* (John 1:14). The embryo in Mary's womb was nothing but the pure Word of God—and it took flesh upon itself.

The Word of God, Jesus Christ, was born in the earth. The Living Word of God (Jesus) was the Word personified—the Word of God in flesh form! *And how did it happen?* A woman dared believe and say that she was the woman: "Yes, I believe You. Behold, You have found her."

The Lord said to me, "My Word will get people healed and filled with the Holy Ghost the same way that the miraculous conception took place! **Any believer can conceive My Word** concerning healing in their spirits, and healing will manifest itself in their physical bodies! They can conceive My Word concerning prosperity of finances, and prosperity will manifest itself in their business affairs. If they will conceive My Word concerning the baptism of the Holy Spirit, it will manifest itself in their spirits.

"Ask and you shall receive. Seek and you shall find. Knock and it shall be opened unto you. Everyone that asks, receives.

"How much more shall the heavenly Father give the Holy Spirit to them that ask Him. When the believers receive My Word in their spirits, it will manifest itself in their physical bodies. *Any* believer can conceive the Word of God and say, 'Behold! I am the man that *His stripes healed!*'

"The miraculous conception came through the God-kind of faith. The faith of God rose in Mary's heart, and she received the Word. She conceived it in her spirit, and it manifested itself in her physical body. The embryo in Mary's womb was the Word of God."

I said to the Lord, "I want You to give me some more references to that because Your Word says, *In the mouth of two or three witnesses every word may be established* (Matt. 18:16).

He brought to my attention 1 Peter 1:23: *Being born again, not of corruptible seed, but of incorruptible, by the word of God, that liveth and abideth for ever.*

The Incorruptible Seed

The Word is incorruptible seed. The seed that the woman conceived was the incorruptible seed. When God prophesied about Eve in Genesis 3, she didn't have the seed, but God said "the seed of the woman." The seed Mary received was the Word. The incorruptible Seed, which lives and abides forever, took upon itself flesh and dwelt among us. **God's Word is incorruptible seed.**

Jesus Christ was born of a virgin through the miraculous conception of faith—the *God-kind* of faith. He was born of the everlasting Word. There was no death in Him.

The reason He had to be born of a virgin was that the bloodline follows the father. In Old Testament days, the entire inheritance followed the father. The life of the flesh is in the blood. (Lev. 17:11.) If the life of the flesh is in the blood, the death of the flesh is in the blood also.

Because Adam sinned, every child born from Adam until now has life and death in his bloodstream. He is going to die if time goes on long enough. But Jesus said, "No man takes My life."

Jesus Christ was a man anointed with the Holy Ghost. Someone said, ''I don't understand why Jesus had to be born on earth. Why didn't God just come down here and destroy the Devil?''

He couldn't do that. It was illegal because God had given dominion over the earth to man. Jesus had to come in the form of a man: with the body of man, with the feelings and abilities of a man. He had to approach the Devil as a man. This made it perfectly legal for Jesus to destroy the works of the Devil.

The immortal words of Jesus were heard throughout all the universe: *The Spirit of the Lord is upon me, because he hath anointed me . . .* (Luke 4:18).

The Word had truly become flesh through the miraculous conception.

The Necessity of the Virgin Birth

Every person born after Adam sinned is born in sin. They have the nature of their illegitimate stepfather, Satan.

Jesus had no earthly father. He was born of a woman. This is what makes the virgin birth a must—the bloodline follows the father. Medical science has found that under normal birth conditions not one drop of blood passes from the mother to the child. They thought for years that the mother furnished blood for the child; now they know this is not so. The blood is formed from the union of the two.

The embryo formed in Mary's womb was the Word of God. Therefore, it produced pure blood, filled with life. God was the Father. Jesus was on earth, born of a virgin, with the blood of God in His veins. The Bible calls Him ''the last Adam.'' If He had an earthly father, He would have had death in His blood. Man is born with both life and death in him. But Jesus' blood was not polluted. There was no death in Him.

Listen to the statements of Jesus. *No man taketh it* (life) *from me, but I lay it down of myself* (John 10:18). *The prince of this world* (Satan) *cometh, and hath nothing in me* (John 14:30).

People tried to kill Jesus several times, but they could not. There was no death in Him. There was no sin in Him. He was filled with *love*!

Jesus was born of a woman, but God's blood flowed in His veins. It had to be so or He could not have been the supreme sacrifice. The sacrifice had to be a man who was perfect. He had the life of God flowing in Him, and He gave it as a sin offering for the world.

If Jesus had not been born of a virgin, you would still be in your sins. It had to be so or redemption could never have become a reality.

Jesus Came to Destroy the Works of the Devil

. . . For this purpose the Son of God was manifested, that he might destroy the works of the devil (1 John 3:8).

The Amplified Bible states: ''. . . The reason the Son of God was made manifest (visible) was to **undo** (destroy, loosen and dissolve) the works the devil [has done].'' Jesus was sent to restore man to his rightful godliness.

At twelve years of age, Jesus astounded religious leaders with His knowledge of the Law. Here was actually the Covenant-making God Who had become a sacrifice Himself!

In Luke, chapter 3, John was baptizing. *And as the people were in expectation, and all men mused in their hearts of John, whether he were the Christ, or not; John answered, saying unto them all, I indeed baptize you with water; but one mightier than I cometh, the latchet of whose shoes I am not worthy to unloose: he shall baptize you with the Holy Ghost and with fire* (vv. 15,16).

Now when all the people were baptized, it came to pass, that Jesus also being baptized, and praying, the heaven was opened, and the Holy Ghost descended in a bodily shape like a dove upon him, and a voice came from heaven, which said, Thou art my beloved Son; in thee I am well pleased. And Jesus himself began to be about thirty years of age, being (as was supposed) the son of Joseph . . . (vv. 21-23).

We know Jesus wasn't the son of Joseph. He was the Son of God. The majority of religious teaching today tells you Jesus healed the sick in order to prove He was the Son of God.

Do you realize that Jesus was thirty years of age when He was baptized? *Until that time, He had not healed one person.* He had not raised anyone from the dead; He had not done one miracle—not one! Surely He was as much the Son of God at age twenty-nine as He was at age thirty.

The real reason Jesus healed the sick, raised the dead, and cast out demons was because *He was anointed with the Holy Ghost to destroy the works of the Devil.*

Jesus didn't heal the sick because of His divine power. He was the Son of God. He was deity. But when He came to earth, **He stripped Himself of His divine power.** He didn't use any power inherent in Him as God's Son to heal the sick, raise the dead, cast out demons, or destroy other works of the Devil.

God Anointed Jesus

Notice that it was *after* the Holy Ghost descended on Jesus in the bodily form of a dove that He began to heal the sick, cast out demons, and perform miracles. We find this account in Acts 10:38: *How God anointed Jesus of Nazareth with the Holy Ghost and with power: who went about doing good, and healing all that were oppressed of the devil: for God was with him.*

Jesus was anointed with the Holy Ghost and healing power. This scripture says oppression, sickness, and disease are of the evil one, the Devil.

The power Jesus used in His ministry was not something He brought from heaven with Him. It wasn't inherent in Him as being the Son of God. The Bible says **God anointed Him.**

If Jesus healed the sick because of His divine power, *why* did God anoint Him? He was God manifested in the flesh. Where would you go to get a higher anointing than God? *It was because of the anointing of God that Jesus healed the sick.*

Jesus came to earth as a man. He did not take the nature of angels nor the nature of God in His divine power. He took on Him the nature of man. Jesus became a man. Jesus continually affirmed, "I am the Son of Man."

There were several occasions when He referred to Himself as being the "Son of God," but He simply referred back to the place where He said, "I and My Father are one," and, "Are you going to stone Me, because I said I am the Son of God?''

Jesus was here with legal authority on earth as a man. He had to be anointed with the Holy Ghost to heal the sick. He was on earth without sin. He could operate perfectly under the Old Covenant—the Abrahamic Covenant. In fact, the promise was not just to Abraham but to Abraham and his Seed. Abraham was capable of operating in it while he was on earth *until the Seed came*. Not *seeds* (as many), but *Seed* (as one) and *that Seed is Christ*.

Abraham simply held that promise until the Seed came. Jesus was born of a virgin. He came into the earth with the blood of God flowing through His veins. Jesus was a perfect specimen of humanity, and He called Himself *the Son of Man*.

The Last Adam

And so it is written, The first man Adam was made a living soul; the last Adam was made a quickening spirit. Howbeit that was not first which is spiritual, but that which is natural; and afterward that which is spiritual. The first man is of the earth, earthy: the second man is the Lord from heaven (1 Cor. 15:45-47).

Jesus was called *the last Adam.* He was made *a quickening spirit.* Many times when Jesus healed the sick, He would say, "Go, and see that you tell no man." If He were trying to prove He was the Son of God by healing the sick, He would have said, "Go tell everybody I am the Son of God."

Jesus was called the Son of Man. The Bible says you will see the Son of Man coming in the clouds of heaven. He will *still* be the Son of *Man* when He comes back. Jesus identifies with man. He came to earth to operate as a man, anointed with the Holy Ghost. Because He was in the earth as a man, He could legally destroy the works of the Devil.

Satan didn't know who Jesus was until the day the Holy Ghost came on Him. In fact, you'll find that John the Baptist began to have doubts also. When John was put into prison, he sent two people to ask Jesus if He was the One to come or should they look for another? Jesus didn't even answer John's question. He simply said, "Go back and tell John what you saw. The blind received their sight; the poor had the Gospel preached to them . . . ." (Luke 7:19,22.)

The Temptation of Jesus

Jesus met Satan on the Mount of Temptation in the power of the Spirit. Here is the Son of Man *in His authority.* After He had fasted forty days, *the devil said unto him, If thou be the Son of God, command this stone that it be made bread. And Jesus answered him, saying, It is written, That man shall not live by bread alone, but by every word of God* (Luke 4:3,4).

Jesus simply quoted what God said. He would not get involved in what *seemed* to be or what *might* be. **He just quoted God's Word.**

And the devil, taking him up into an high mountain, shewed unto him all the kingdoms of the world in a moment of time. And the devil said unto him, All this power will I give thee, and the glory of them: for that is delivered unto me; and to whomsoever I will give it (vv. 5,6).

Evidently, Satan knew that Jesus had come to restore man. Satan didn't understand it all because he is spiritually dead; but he had a general idea of what Jesus was going to do to him. He said, "I'll give it back to You if You will worship me."

*And Jesus answered and said unto him, Get thee behind me, Satan: **for it is written,** Thou shalt worship the Lord thy God, and him only shalt thou serve. And he brought him to Jerusalem, and set him on a pinnacle of the temple, and said unto him, If thou be the Son of God, cast thyself down from hence* (vv. 8,9).

Here was Jesus' chance to prove He was the Son of God, but that was not what He came to do. Jesus came to "undo (destroy, loosen and dissolve) the works of the devil." He didn't get caught up in proving that He was the Son of God. Jesus didn't need to prove anything: time would prove that.

Satan did challenge Jesus: "*If* You be the Son of God . . . ." Notice Satan himself started quoting Scripture. (The Devil knows a few scriptures, but he quotes them out of context.) *For it is written, He shall give his angels charge over thee, to keep thee: and in their hands they shall bear thee up, lest at any time thou dash thy foot against a stone* (v. 10). (He quoted it well, but took it out of context.)

And Jesus answering said unto him, It is said, Thou shalt not tempt the Lord thy God. And when the devil had ended all the temptation, he departed from him for a season (Luke 4:12,13).

Jesus spoke three words that shook Satan's kingdom beyond repair—**It is written!**

8
The Authority of the Body

And he came to Nazareth, where he had been brought up: and, as his custom was, he went into the synagogue on the sabbath day, and stood up for to read.

And there was delivered unto him the book of the prophet Esaias. And when he had opened the book, he found the place where it was written,

The Spirit of the Lord is upon me, because he hath anointed me to preach the gospel to the poor; he hath sent me to heal the brokenhearted, to preach deliverance to the captives, and recovering of sight to the blind, to set at liberty them that are bruised, to preach the acceptable year of the Lord.

And he closed the book, and he gave it again to the minister, and sat down. And the eyes of all them that were in the synagogue were fastened on him.

And he began to say unto them, This day is this scripture fulfilled in your ears . . .

And all they in the synagogue, when they heard these things, were filled with wrath, and rose up, and thrust him out of the city, and led him unto the brow of the hill whereon their city was built, that they might cast him down headlong.

But he passing through the midst of them went his way, and came down to Capernaum, a city of Galilee, and taught them on the sabbath days.

Luke 4:16-21; 28-31

Jesus walked into the synagogue that day in His own hometown. It was the first sermon He ever preached, and the Jews tried to kill Him. They were so angry because Jesus said, *The Spirit of the Lord is upon me, because he hath anointed me to preach the gospel.*

They didn't believe Jesus was anointed to preach the Gospel (the Good News). Good news to the poor is: You don't have to be poor anymore! He said that the blind didn't have to be blind anymore, that the broken-hearted didn't need to be broken-hearted anymore! The bruised didn't have to be bruised! Jesus came preaching *Good News!*

I am convinced that if Jesus had said, "Well, everybody has to be sick sometime. You will never have anything on the earth; you'll have to wait until you get to heaven. You will have to suffer trials and tribulations that come your way. There's nothing you can do about it . . . ," they would have said, "Amen, Brother! We're going to vote you in as pastor!"

But Jesus came preaching the truth—the Good News! He said He was anointed. If Jesus was there in His divine power, why did He have to be anointed?

Jesus entered the earth legally because He was born here. He was born of a virgin; the blood of God flowed through His veins. He was the Son of Man; yet He was God manifested in the flesh.

A literal translation of Philippians 2:7,8 says that when Jesus came to earth, He stripped Himself of that divine power and became a man.

Acts 10:38 tells us that He was anointed with the Holy Ghost and with power, and went about doing good, healing all who were oppressed by the Devil; for God was with Him.

First John 3:8 says, . . . *For this purpose the Son of God was manifested, that he might destroy the works of the devil.* Jesus came to earth to get back everything Satan had stolen from Adam.

Yes, Jesus was the Son of God. Yes, He was deity in this earth. But He did not operate in divine power. **He performed miracles by the anointing of the Holy Ghost—the same Holy Ghost that is available to you and me today!**

A Legal Body

Let's look at the legal aspect of being born in the earth. Understanding the authority God has given man is of utmost importance.

Verily, verily, I say unto you, He that entereth not by the door into the sheepfold, but climbeth up some other way, the same is a thief and a robber. But he that entereth in by the door is the shepherd of the sheep (John 10:1,2).

I stopped one day as I was reading this scriptural passage and said, "Now, Lord, I'd like for You to reveal what that means. I've looked at it for years. I don't understand it. What is *the sheepfold?*"

He answered, "The sheepfold is the earth. My Word says you are the sheep of My pasture. You're not in heaven yet, are you? The door represents the legal entry. Any being coming into the earth any other way than through the legal entry (door) is a thief and a robber."

I asked, "But what is the door, or the legal entry, into the earth?"

He said, *"The legal entry is being born in the earth of a woman.* He that enters not into the earth by being born here, but by attaining entrance some other way, the same is a thief and a robber and **he does not have legal authority on earth.**

"Satan is the one who's here illegally. He climbed up some other way—he wasn't born here and has no right to be here. He is the thief and the robber."

A thief robbing the First National Bank may have *power* when he's holding a gun on people, demanding their money, but he has no *authority*. Satan has been stealing from you, and he has no authority to do so! But if you are born here, you have legal authority. That is *Good News* to everyone on earth!

To him the porter openeth; and the sheep hear his voice: and he calleth his own sheep by name, and leadeth them out (v. 3). This is the purpose of Jesus coming to earth: to lead us out of the darkness into the light, and eventually out of this world into a new heaven and a new earth.

Out of His own mouth, Jesus revealed some of the greatest truths of the Bible.

The thief cometh not, but for to steal, and to kill, and to destroy (v. 10).

Verily, verily, I say unto you, He that entereth not by the door into the sheepfold, but climbeth up some other way, the same is a thief and a robber (v. 1). The thief was not born here. He entered this earth illegally for the purpose of stealing, killing, and destroying.

Legal Authority

Jesus said to Nicodemus, *That which is born of flesh is flesh; and that which is born of the Spirit is spirit* (John 3:6).

That ought to tell us something. We are born, first, of the flesh; then, of the Spirit. Beings who are born here have authority in the earth.

Jesus said, . . . *I am come that they might have life, and that they might have it more abundantly* (v. 10). *He that entereth in by the door is the shepherd of the sheep* (v. 2). Jesus has come that we might have life and have it more abundantly. It is Jesus Who entered by the door and is the Shepherd of the sheep!

He didn't say, "I am come that ye might have tribulations, and that ye might have them more often!" No! He came that we might have abundant life. Jesus came to undo, destroy, and dissolve the works of the Devil.

We see a great truth: **Only people born on earth have authority here.** God delegated the first authority to Adam, but Adam turned it over to Satan. Satan entered this earth illegally. But Jesus has come that we may have life. He has come to destroy and take away those things Satan perpetrated upon man. He came to restore man to his rightful authority.

Jesus Is the Door

When Adam became subordinate to Satan, he was born from life unto death. Jesus came to reverse that process and

cause man *to be born from death unto life!*
Jesus was the last Adam; there won't be
another. **He obtained eternal
redemption for us!**

*And a stranger will they not follow, but
will flee from him: for they know not the
voice of strangers. This parable spake Jesus
unto them: but they understood not what
things they were which he spake unto them.
Then said Jesus unto them again, Verily,
verily, I say unto you, I am the door . . .*
(John 10:5-7).

From the time Jesus says, *He that
entereth in by the door is the shepherd of the
sheep,* He talks about going before us to
lead us out. All that Jesus did for us, the
cross and all, is between those Scripture
verses just before you get to the
statement, *I am the door.*

I couldn't understand it. I kept
trying to say the two doors were the
same, but they were not. The first door
is a legal entry through physical birth,
being born of a woman. It gives us
authority here. The second door is the
spiritual birth, *being born of the Spirit.*

Jesus told Nicodemus, "**You must
be born again.** That which is born of
flesh is flesh; that which is born of the

Spirit is spirit." (John 3:3-6.) Even though man is legally born in the earth, he is a child of the Devil and must be born again from spiritual *death* to spiritual *life*.

Jesus, The Way

Jesus said He was the door and all that ever came before Him were thieves and robbers. Many religious systems claim to be "the way," but they are *not*. There is only one way to heaven. It's not through a church door. It's through Jesus—*the* door! **Jesus is the way!**

You may go to church in order to get to Jesus, but He's not talking about a church door. He's saying the *only* way is coming through *Him*, Jesus Christ. He is the door, and if you don't go through that door, you're not going to make it. You can't climb up the backstairs!

Demons and evil spirits came into the earth illegally by climbing up the back way, but **you're not going to get into heaven any other way except through the door, which is Jesus. He is the door of the sheep.**

While Jesus was on earth, He kept saying He was going to die and rise again. The people didn't understand, but He kept telling them.

. . . the prince of this world cometh, and hath nothing in me (John 14:30). There was nothing in Jesus that Satan could get hold of. Jesus called Satan *the prince of this world*, then said, *but he hath nothing in me.* Satan couldn't get hold of His words because Jesus quoted the Word of God.

In John 10:15 Jesus said, *As the Father knoweth me, even so know I the Father: and I lay down my life for the sheep.* (Notice, *I lay down my life for the sheep.*)

Therefore doth my father love me, because I lay down my life, that I might take it again. No man taketh it from me (vv. 17,18).

I emphasize His words: *No man taketh it from me.* No man could take Jesus' life. They tried to several times while He was on earth; but He simply walked out from their midst. The anointing of God was on Jesus so strong that none could lay hold on Him.

No man taketh it from me, but I lay it down of myself. I have power to lay it down, and I have power to take it again.

This commandment have I received of my Father (v. 18).

Jesus made the decision to give His life while still on earth, while in the Garden of Gethsemane. Jesus prayed a prayer in the Garden that will make your hair stand on end if you read it with the thought of *eternal redemption* at stake.

He prayed, *Abba, Father, all things are possible unto thee; take away this cup from me . . .* (Mark 14:36). **Take away this cup from me!** Jesus never prayed a prayer that was not answered. Here, the humanity of Jesus is showing through.

"All things are possible with thee, so take away this cup from me." **What if Jesus had stopped there and walked off?** But He *didn't*, thank God!

Nevertheless not what I will, but what thou wilt. Oh, what a difference the word *nevertheless* makes in His prayer! This was a prayer of dedication. Jesus had decided to go with God's plan! He made the choice. "I'm going to lay down My life." *Jesus gave His life; no one took it from Him.*

Listen to the words of Jesus: *When I was daily with you in the temple, ye stretched forth no hands against me: but this is your hour, and the power of darkness* (Luke 22:53).

These are the words of a man—the man, Jesus, the Son of God—on His way to such a horrible death. *This is your hour, and the power of darkness.* He has given Himself *to be the sin offering for all men;* then *to become sin* that we might have eternal redemption.

9
The Authority of Jesus

The authority of Jesus and His unity
with the Father is clearly established in
John 10:30. *I and my Father are one.*

*Then the Jews took up stones again to
stone him.*

*Jesus answered them, Many good works
have I shewed you from my Father; for
which of those works do ye stone me?*

*The Jews answered him, saying, For a
good work we stone thee not; but for
blasphemy; and because that thou, being a
man, makest thyself God.*

*Jesus answered them, Is it not written in
your law, I said, Ye are gods?* (John
10:31-34).

The Amplified Bible says of verse 33,
. . because You, a mere man, make
Yourself [out to be] God.''

Continuing from the *King James
Version:*

*Jesus answered them, Is it not written in
your law, I said, Ye are gods? If he called*

*them gods, unto whom the word of God
came, and the scripture cannot be broken;*

*Say ye of him, whom the Father hath
sanctified, and sent into the world, Thou
blasphemest; because I said, I am the Son of
God?* (vv. 34-36).

When Jesus mentioned that man
was created to be a god over the earth,
He was quoting from Psalm 82:1. *God
standeth in the congregation of the mighty;
he judgeth among the gods.*

The translators, for fear of getting
themselves in trouble, translated this
"congregation of the mighty" while the
correct word is *elohim,* the plural for *god.*
"God standeth in the congregation of
the *elohim,*" and, "He judgeth among
the gods (or the *elohim*)." They didn't
know what to do with the word *elohim,*
so they translated it "mighty." They
didn't know what He was really saying,
that man was created to be god over this
earth.

Someone might say, "Well, He is
talking about the Trinity—Father, Son,
and Holy Ghost."

That might sound good until you
read verses 2 and 3. *How long will ye
judge unjustly, and accept the persons of the*

wicked? . . . Defend the poor and fatherless: do justice to the afflicted and needy.

If He is talking about the Father, Son, and Holy Ghost, He would be accusing the Holy Ghost and God of being unjust. But He is talking about **man.** He calls him *elohim*, created in the image and likeness of God. God duplicated Himself in kind. Man was created to have dominion and authority in the earth. It was *Elohim* among the *elohim*.

Paul says in Ephesians 3:14,15, *I bow my knees unto the Father of our Lord Jesus Christ, of whom the whole family in heaven and earth is named.*

Notice, it isn't one family in heaven and another one in earth. We are the family of God—*Elohim* among the *elohim*. Man needs to return to his rightful place and see himself as the Creator created him!

*They know not, neither will they understand; they walk on in darkness: all the foundations of the earth are out of course. I have said, **Ye are gods;** and all of you are children of the most High* (Ps. 82:5,6).

The foundations of the earth are out of course. Satan has perverted the course of nature.

Ye are gods; and all of you are children of the most High. But ye shall die like men, and fall like one of the princes. Arise, O God, judge the earth: for thou shalt inherit all nations (Ps. 82:6-8).

Demons Challenge
The Authority of Jesus

We find that the authority of Jesus came from His being legally born in the earth. Then, at age thirty, He was anointed with the Holy Ghost so that He could undo, loosen, and dissolve the works of the Devil. He was the last Adam. Jesus had the authority of a man while God furnished the anointing and power.

We read Luke 4:33,34 where Jesus' authority is challenged. *And in the synagogue there was a man, which had a spirit of an unclean devil, and cried out with a loud voice, saying, Let us alone; what have we to do with thee, thou Jesus of Nazareth? art thou come to destroy us? I know thee who thou art; the Holy One of God.*

The religious leaders wanted to kill Jesus, but the demons recognized Him: "We know who you are: the Holy One of God."

It shocked the regions of the damned when they saw Jesus destroying the works of the Devil. The demons challenged Jesus' authority in the earth. Demons knew it was illegal for God to come to earth in His divine power and destroy the works of the Devil.

Satan had become the god of the world system. Demons challenged Jesus because they thought they had authority here. They came against Jesus by saying, "We know Who You are, so let us alone! You don't have authority to do this, because *You* are *God*. We know Who You are, and You can't do this."

Jesus said, "Shut your mouth and come out of him." And they did! Now if there was any doubt about who has greater authority here, that should settle it! **Jesus was operating as a *man*, anointed with the Holy Ghost.**

And when he was come to the other side into the country of the Gergesenes, there met him two possessed with devils, coming out of the tombs, exceeding fierce, so that no man might pass by that way. And, behold, they cried out, saying, What have we to do with thee, Jesus, thou Son of God? art thou

come hither to torment us before the time?
(Matt. 8:28,29).

Notice that demons know a time is
coming when they will be destroyed.
They said, "It's not time yet, and You
can't do that." Jesus said only one
word, "Go!" and they went.

Adam's Lease on the Earth

There is a day coming that Satan will
be bound for 1,000 years. But until
man's lease on the earth runs out, God
is limited in what He can do about the
Devil.

Evidently, God gave Adam a 6,000-
year lease on earth. At the end of that
time, there is to be 1,000 years of rest.

Peter said, *Be not ignorant of this one
thing, that one day is with the Lord as a
thousand years, and a thousand years as one
day* (2 Pet. 3:8). Now, don't try to use
that every time the word *day* is used,
because it won't fit!

But here is something you need to
see. With the Lord, a day is as 1,000
years and 1,000 years is as a day. The
context is found in the first chapter of
Genesis. I believe the whole plan of
redemption is there, from beginning to

end. For example, on the sixth day God created man in His own image and in His own likeness. I don't believe a day of creation was 1,000 years. The Scriptures prove that wrong.

Yet, there is a parallel here. Man was created the sixth day. He came into the likeness of God on the last day of creation. It is in the 6,000th year that man will come into the likeness of what he was created to be. I'm not saying all men are getting better. No! Wicked men will get worse, but the Body of Christ will come into perfection on this last day.

The seventh day, or the 7,000th year, shall begin the 1,000 years of rest, for Satan will be bound 1,000 years. This is the *rest* for the people of God. (Heb. 4:3-9.)

The Lease on the Vineyard

And he began to speak unto them by parables. A certain man planted a vineyard, and set an hedge about it, and digged a place for the winefat, and built a tower, and let it out to husbandmen, and went into a far country (Mark 12:1).

Jesus is portraying a lease on the earth. God created the earth for Adam. He hedged it about and gave Adam complete authority in that he would be total ruler of this earth. Adam could do what he wanted with it. It was totally delivered to Adam.

And at the season he sent to the husbandmen a servant, that he might receive from the husbandmen of the fruit of the vineyard. And they caught him, and beat him, and sent him away empty.

And again he sent unto them another servant; and at him they cast stones, and wounded him in the head, and sent him away shamefully handled. And again he sent another; and him they killed, and many others; beating some and killing some.

Having yet therefore one son, his wellbeloved, he sent him also last unto them, saying, They will reverence my son. But those husbandmen said among themselves, This is the heir; come, let us kill him, and the inheritance shall be ours.

And they took him, and killed him, and cast him out of the vineyard.

What shall therefore the lord of the vineyard do? he will come and destroy the husbandmen, and will give the vineyard unto others (vv. 2-9).

The husbandmen are the people of the earth inspired of the evil one, Satan. It is really a reflection of what Satan was saying about Jesus. "Look. He is the heir. If we can kill this Son and get Him out of the way, the inheritance is ours!"

That is why Satan rejoiced when Jesus died the deaths. He said, "We will annihilate the Son of God, and *all* will be ours! He is the last Adam; there will be no more after Him. The whole earth is ours!" **But God had other plans!**

There is a time set. Satan and his demons know there is a day of reckoning coming. So they challenged Jesus. "Have You come to destroy us before our time?" In other words, "You can't do that yet. It's not time!"

They challenged Jesus' authority because they didn't understand the virgin birth. They didn't know what God had done to make Jesus' entry into the earth legal. It was His appearance as a man that gave Jesus the authority to destroy the works of the Devil *legally!*

Your Body Is the Temple of God

The reason Satan hates your body is because it's the temple of the Holy Ghost. Your body is the only temple God has on earth today. It gives you authority. Satan does not have a physical body and has no *legal* right here. He is a created being and spiritually dead. Jesus had the body of a man and the authority of a man. The ability to destroy the works of the Devil came through the anointing of the Holy Ghost.

There is a difference between *delegated authority* and *ability*. Men have authority in the earth but don't have the ability to do the works that Jesus did. It is through the anointing of the Holy Ghost that the ability of God flows through man.

God uses His ability and power to destroy the Devil's works, but He channels it through those that are *born here*.

Jesus faced a challenge of His authority. Demons thought He was destroying Satan's work on earth because He was God. But His authority came from being a man born on earth;

His ability came from the anointing of the Holy Ghost.

*For as the Father hath life in himself; so hath he given to the Son to have life in himself; and hath given him authority to execute judgment also, **because he is the Son of man*** (John 5:26,27). Jesus had authority, not because He was God's Son, but because He was the Son of Man.

The word *authority* means "lawful permission to execute power, or ability to bring judgment or justice for or against." Jesus had full power as a man and the ability of God to execute judgment *for* use and *against* the Devil.

Satan Was Baffled

When Jesus was born in Bethlehem, Satan couldn't understand the "big to-do." Angels were running through the sky proclaiming, "There's a Savior born which is Christ the Lord!"

Satan probably thought, *Big deal! I'll cut Him down to size!* But he forgot one thing: God now had, for Himself, a man-child on earth—the Son of God stripped of His divine power; but soon to be anointed with the Holy Ghost and power. Satan soon found he was no match for Jesus or the Covenant.

Jesus Is Challenged Again

And they come again to Jerusalem: and as he was walking in the temple, there come to him the chief priests, and the scribes, and the elders, and say unto him, By what authority doest thou these things? and who gave thee this authority to do these things? (Mark 11:27,28):

Not only did demons challenge Jesus, but also the religious leaders. "Where did *You* get this authority?" That question was demon inspired. Those men didn't know that legal authority belonged to those born on earth.

Notice the two questions they asked:

1. *By what authority doest thou these things?*

2. *Who gave thee this authority?*

The Devil wanted the answers, so he moved the religious leaders to find out for him.

And Jesus answered and said unto them, I will also ask of you one question, and answer me, and I will tell you by what author-

ity I do these things. The baptism of John was it from heaven, or of men? answer me.

And they reasoned with themselves, saying, If we shall say, From heaven; he will say, Why then did ye not believe him? But if we shall say, Of men; they feared the people: for all men counted John, that he was a prophet indeed.

And they answered and said unto Jesus, We cannot tell. And Jesus answering saith unto them, Neither do I tell you by what authority I do these things.

Mark 11:29-33

I was meditating on this one day and knew there was something I had missed. The Lord said to me, "I was going to use their own words to answer their questions. They asked Me two questions. If they had answered My question, it would have answered both of theirs."

Remember when they asked Jesus, "Is it lawful to pay tribute to Caesar?" Jesus told them to bring Him a penny. When He asked, *Whose is this image and superscription?* (Mark 12:16), they answered, *Caesar's.* Then He said to them, *Render to Caesar the things that are*

Caesar's, and to God the things that are God's (v. 17).

This is exactly what Jesus was about to do in this situation. But the leaders became fearful and decided it was a trick to turn the Jews against them, so they said, "We cannot tell."

The true answer was that John's baptism was of both man and God. John's baptism was of *man*, but John was sent from *God*. The baptism was the baptism of repentance, but was not from heaven.

John himself said, "There comes one after me that shall baptize you with the Holy Ghost and with fire." (Luke 3:16.)

The Holy Ghost baptism is the baptism from heaven. John was not a born-again man, and the people he baptized were not born again. It was a baptism of repentance; it was man's baptism. It was a step in the right direction and was the best afforded under the Old covenant, but it was of men.

Therefore Jesus would have answered, "I do these things by the *authority* gained by being a *man* born on earth, and *God* gave Me the *power* through the *anointing* of the Holy Ghost!''

The authority of Jesus came from being born as a man. His power and anointing came from God.

10
Judgment of this World

When he putteth forth his own sheep, he goeth before them and the sheep follow him: for they know his voice (John 10:4).

Jesus' primary purpose in coming to earth was to destroy the Devil's works. He was willing to use whatever means it took to do that.

I want you to see what Jesus did to redeem mankind: how He went before *you* to the cross; how He suffered *the full curse of the Law* which is poverty, sickness, and spiritual death, for *you*; how He became sin and suffered *in your place*—one of the most awesome truths of the Bible.

In the Garden, Jesus said, *My soul is exceeding sorrowful unto death* (Mark 14:34). Here you realize there's something in Jesus' mind other than physical death. He certainly was not afraid to die physically.

He was suffering the thoughts of the separation from His Father that He knew was soon to come. He was about to take what should have been coming to mankind, and this would separate Him from His Father. This was the part that was so horrible: **the separation from God.** He was to become sin. He wrestled with it until blood came through His pores and dropped to the ground.

And he taketh with him Peter and James and John, and began to be sore amazed, and to be very heavy; and saith unto them, My soul is exceeding sorrowful unto death: tarry ye here, and watch.

And he went forward a little, and fell on the ground, and prayed that, if it were possible, the hour might pass from him.

And he said, Abba, Father, all things are possible unto thee; take away this cup from me: nevertheless not what I will, but what thou wilt.

And he cometh, and findeth them sleeping, and saith unto Peter, Simon, sleepest thou? couldest not thou watch one hour? Watch ye and pray, lest ye enter into temptation. The spirit truly is ready, but the flesh is weak.

And again he went away, and prayed, and spake the same words. And when he returned, he found them asleep again, (for their eyes were heavy,) neither wist they what to answer him.

And he cometh the third time, and saith unto them, Sleep on now, and take your rest: it is enough, the hour is come; behold, the Son of man is betrayed into the hands of sinners.

Mark 14:33-41

Jesus Gave Himself

There was no way Satan could get a hold on Jesus. There was *no sin* in Him. Satan could not lay any kind of claim to Him. The blood of God flowed in His veins. Jesus was a union of the *Word of God* and *human flesh.*

When the time came for Jesus to be betrayed, He said, *Now is the judgment of this world: now shall the prince of this world be cast out* (John 12:31).

The Greek word for *judgment* is *krisis*, meaning "turning point." The English word closest in meaning is *crisis*. So Jesus was saying, "Now the crisis, or turning point, has come, and

I'm going to cast the prince of this world out!"

. . . My kingdom is not of this world: if my kingdom were of this world, then would my servants fight, that I should not be delivered to the Jews (John 18:36).

Jesus knew He was on His way to the cross as He said, "Satan cometh but he hath nothing in Me," and "No man takes My life; I lay it down of Myself."

Hear the prophetic words of Pilate, *I have found no cause of death in him* (Luke 23:22). I am sure Pilate did not understand the twofold meaning of his prophetic utterance. Jesus had to be without spot. There could be no sacrifice offered that was blemished or had any cause of death in Him.

The satanic forces were rejoicing that Jesus had been delivered up. After a mock trial, the Son of God was sentenced illegally and crucified. Jesus had given Himself up to the Father's plan. He was nailed to the cross. As He hung there, suspended between heaven and earth, darkness covered the land for three hours.

Who hath believed our report? and to whom is the arm of the Lord revealed? For he

*shall grow up before him as a tender plant,
and as a root out of a dry ground: he hath no
form nor comeliness; and when we shall see
him, there is no beauty that we should desire
him. He is despised and rejected of men; a
man of sorrows, and acquainted with grief:
. . . and we esteemed him not.*

*Surely he hath borne our griefs, and
carried our sorrows: yet we did esteem him
stricken, smitten of God, and afflicted. But
he was wounded for our trangressions, he
was bruised for our iniquities: the
chastisement of our peace was upon him;
and with his stripes we are healed.*

Isaiah 53:1-5

The Hebrew word translated *grief*
means "sickness." The Hebrew says,
"He bore our sickness and carried our
pains."

In *The Amplified Bible* verse 5 reads,
"But he was wounded for our transgressions, He was bruised for our guilt
and iniquities; the chastisement needful
to obtain peace and well-being for us
was upon Him, and with the stripes
that wounded Him we are healed and
made whole."

I want you to notice verse 5. *He was
wounded for our transgressions, he was*

bruised for our iniquities. The word *bruised* is the very same word that is translated "stripes," found later in the verse. When these two words were translated, one was translated "bruised," the other, "stripes." This was done in order to keep from repeating.

Here is the key to understanding healing in the Atonement. The bruises that were placed upon Jesus to deliver you from your sins and iniquities are the *same* bruises that took care of your sicknesses and diseases. There weren't bruises for one and stripes for the other. They were the same bruises, and you can't separate them.

Today some people say, "You can be saved and have your sins forgiven, but God doesn't heal anymore."

But wait a minute! The same bruises that set you free from your iniquities also healed you and brought deliverance to your body.

So let's read it that way: *He was bruised for our iniquities: the chastisement of our peace was upon him; and with his bruises we are healed.* We are healed with the same bruises.

Now let's read it in *The Amplified Bible*. "But He was wounded for our transgressions, He was bruised for our guilt and iniquities; the chastisement needful to obtain peace and well-being for us was upon Him, and with the *stripes* that wounded Him *we are healed and made whole*." We can also say, "With the *bruises* that wounded Him we are healed and made whole."

The bruises that took your iniquities away are the same bruises that healed your body. As far as God is concerned, it was all done at the same time nearly 2,000 years ago.

Dual Death

In Isaiah 53:9, we find these awesome words: *And he made his grave with the wicked, and with the rich in his death; because he had done no violence, neither was any deceit in his mouth.*

The Hebrew word for *death* is plural—not *one* death, but *two*. "He made his grave with the wicked in his *deaths*."

For he hath made him to be sin for us, who knew no sin; that we might be made the righteousness of God in him (2 Cor. 5:21).

No! Jesus did not become a *sinner*!
He became sin! He took *our* sin upon
Himself and bore those sins away.

Hebrews 9:12 tells us *by his own blood
he* (Jesus) *entered in once into the holy
place, having obtained **eternal redemption**
for us.* Jesus became sin that we might
be righteous—that we would no more
be separated from God—that we might
have eternal redemption!

The spirits of men are eternal. (Your
spirit is eternal.) There was something
eternal at stake when mankind was
spiritually dead. You must realize that
for Jesus to go before us and prepare the
way, He had to redeem man from
spiritual death.

There was only one way to do this:
He had to suffer the penalty of sin (*the
soul that sinneth, it shall die*). But Jesus
did not sin! Jesus was holy. He went
before us to receive that which we were
about to receive, that which was due us.
Jesus did not sin, but He *received sin*.
There is a difference.

Jesus did not sin. He was holy. He
went before us and received that which
we should have suffered. He became

sin, so that we could receive eternal redemption!

Now you can understand *why* He sweat drops of blood in the Garden. As He hung suspended between heaven and earth on the cross, He released Himself. ''No man takes My life; I lay it down of Myself.''

Jesus opened Himself and received death. The Holy One of God, the Son of God, became *your substitute!* Most of the Church has never seen what Jesus suffered in order to bring life to the lost.

And at the ninth hour Jesus cried with a loud voice, saying, Eloi, Eloi, lama sabach thani? which is, being interpreted, My God, my God, why hast thou forsaken me? (Mark 15:34).

There was no help from God Who chose not to look upon Jesus as He cried out. Jesus could have called more than twelve legions of angels, but He didn't. Instead, He became the sin offering. Then He became a curse.

The trap was set for Satan to move in on Jesus. No doubt Satan thought He must have sinned as men cursed Him, slapped Him, crowned His head with thorns, and lashed His back until it became as a piece of raw meat. Satan thought, *He has surely sinned now.*

No! Jesus never sinned at any time! But, He was about to become sin for you!

Isaiah Prophesied Jesus' Death

The prophet Isaiah saw events which prompted him to say, *Behold, my servant shall deal prudently, he shall be exalted and extolled, and be very high. As many were astonied at thee; his visage was so marred more than any man, and his form more than the sons of men* (Is. 52:13,14).

Isaiah saw it through spiritual revelation. He wasn't there when it happened. Not even people standing around the cross could see all of Jesus' suffering. It was dark for three hours. Jesus' body was drawn in every contortion of pain that disease and sickness could cause.

There was no light. They did not bring their lanterns in the middle of the day. I am convinced every diabolical disease known to man ravaged Jesus' body as He hung on the cross. I believe this was one reason it was dark for three hours: Men could not have stood to look upon humanity in such suffering. He had to suffer the full curse. It was beyond human conception the things Jesus suffered on the cross.

Jesus never suffered sickness on earth until He received every disease that affects mankind as He hung on the cross. Isaiah said His countenance was marred beyond human imagination, worse than any man. Imagine the most twisted, torn, pain-filled man you have ever seen. Jesus was worse than that.

Yet it pleased the Lord to bruise him; he hath put him to grief (Is. 53:10).

". . . although He had done no violence, neither was any deceit in His mouth. Yet it was the will of the Lord to bruise Him; He has put Him to grief and made him sick . . ." (vv. 9,10 AMP).

God made Jesus sick. Why? It was because the chastisement or punishment needful to obtain peace and well-being **for you and me** was upon Jesus. He suffered sickness and punishment so we would not have to!

When did God make Jesus sick? When He made Jesus an offering for sin. *Himself took our infirmities, and bare our sicknesses* (Matt. 8:17). He received every diabolical disease known to man.

Yet it pleased the Lord to bruise him; he hath put him to grief: when thou shalt make his soul an offering for sin, he shall see his seed, he shall prolong his days, and the pleasure of the Lord shall prosper in his hand.

He shall see of the travail of his soul, and shall be satisfied: by his knowledge shall my righteous servant justify many; for he shall bear their iniquities. Therefore will I divide him a portion with the great, and he shall divide the spoil with the strong . . . (Is. 53:10-12).

He's calling us strong! He has divided the spoil with us! The Bible says He spoiled principalities and powers. He made a show of them openly.

. . . because he hath poured out his soul unto death: and he was numbered with the transgressors; and he bare the sins of many, and made intercession for the transgressors. Yes! Thank God! He made intercession for us!

With His Stripes We Are Healed

Let's recap just a little. In Isaiah 53:4 we read, *Surely he hath borne our griefs and carried our sorrows.* (This literally reads, "Surely He has borne our sicknesses and carried our pain.") Jesus of Nazareth did that for us. He suffered every disease and sickness known to mankind. He bore both sickness and grief for us.

You need to know this and *act* on it! The Devil has been putting it on people all these years. He's been giving people flu and other sickness and has conned Christians into believing it's been God teaching them something!

Jesus bore our sicknesses so that we wouldn't have to be sick! He bore our diseases so that we don't have to! Get a revelation of that! This doesn't mean you'll never have diseases just because you read, hear, or have the knowledge that Jesus bore them for you. **If you don't act upon what you know, you'll just go ahead and be sick.**

Every individual must *exercise his authority* and *apply himself* to the Word of God. Just knowing or hearing about what Jesus freed you from is not enough! You have to walk in God's Word and apply it in your life.

Jesus Christ of Nazareth died for **you.** He died two deaths there—

physical and spiritual. He opened Himself and received sin.

God made Jesus to be sin. No, He didn't just *pay* the penalty for sin. He literally *became* sin. He opened Himself *by His words.* Before He died, He said, . . . *Father, into thy hands I commend my spirit* (Luke 23:46).

It was the spiritual part, the human spirit, of Jesus which bore that sin away into an uninhabitable place. Jesus went to hell. **He suffered hell for us so that we won't have to!**

And he made his grave with the wicked, and with the rich in his death (Is. 53:9). The word for *death* here is plural: *two*, not *one* death. But first, the sin offering was made. **The sin offering came first.** Jesus—holy, sinless, and perfect—was the sin offering.

David Prophesied It

The Psalmist David also tapped into what would happen, through prophecy, hundreds of years before Jesus died for humanity. *My God, my God, why hast thou forsaken me? why art thou so far from helping me, and from the words of my roaring?* (Ps. 22:1).

Not many people have seen this. Some deny it, but that doesn't make it any less true. There is no doubt that these are the words of Jesus.

But I am a worm, and no man; a reproach of men, and despised of the people. All they that see me laugh me to scorn: they shoot out the lip, they shake the head, saying, He trusted on the Lord that he would deliver him: let him deliver him, seeing he delighted in him (vv. 6-8).

They gaped upon me with their mouths, as a ravening and a roaring lion. I am poured out like water, and all my bones are out of joint (vv. 13,14).

No doubt arthritis had swollen every joint of His body until every bone was out of joint! Jesus was receiving the chastisement *for our peace.* It was upon Him. The physical punishment needful to satisfy divine justice, to bring peace, and well-being to us was placed upon Jesus, and He bore it *all* for us.

Jesus suffered so you might be healed and walk free from the curse.

. . . My heart is like wax; it is melted in the midst of my bowels. My strength is dried up like a potsherd; and my tongue cleaveth

*to my jaws; and thou hast brought me into
the dust of death.*

*For dogs have compassed me: the
assembly of the wicked have inclosed me:
they pierced my hands and my feet. I may
tell all my bones* (Heb.: "I can see all my
bones"), *they look and stare upon me* (vv.
14-17).

He is saying, "I can see all My
bones." The bones were protruding
outward, pushing the flesh out. His
bones were all out of joint. No
eyewitness verified this in the New
Testament since darkness covered earth
for three hours. Only revelation of God
through prophecy brought it forth.

*They part my garments among them,
and cast lots upon my vesture* (v. 18).

*I will declare thy name unto my
brethren: in the midst of the congregation
will I praise thee* (v. 22).

*All they that be fat upon earth shall eat
and worship: all they that go down to the
dust shall bow before him: and none can
keep alive his own soul. A seed shall serve
him; it shall be accounted to the Lord for a
generation. They shall come, and shall
declare his righteousness unto a people
that shall be born, that he hath done this*

(vv. 29-31). (The literal translation is "that it is finished.")

As Jesus hung on the cross, He said, *It is finished* (John 19:30). Many Bible scholars believe Jesus quoted the whole Twenty-second Psalm as He hung on the cross. When He said, "It is finished," He didn't mean God's plan for redemption was finished. He was saying that **the last sacrifice to be offered under the Old Covenant was finished.** The Law was fulfilled.

There will never be another sacrifice accepted by God; works or good deeds won't be received. **Jesus was the only sacrifice for redemption!**

Jesus Made His Grave With the Wicked

Isaiah prophesied, *And he made his grave with the wicked, and with the rich in his death*(s) (Is. 53:9).

Man has looked at this scripture through religious eyeglasses and said, "Yes, Jesus was buried in the tomb of the rich man." But that's not what Isaiah said. Jesus made the decision to make His grave with the wicked in His deaths. (He hung on the cross with the wicked, then went to hell.)

In that day when lost people died, they went to the abode of the wicked dead. After the atonement for sin (sin offering) was made, Jesus was made to be sin and went to the place of the wicked dead. He made His grave in hell with the wicked and rich in His deaths.

I asked the Lord, "What *rich* was Isaiah talking about?"

He said, "The rich man in the 16th chapter of Luke."

In that day the abode of the righteous was in a separate compartment across from the wicked dead. In the 16th chapter of Luke, we find that the beggar was in Abraham's bosom. The rich man in hell could look over and see him, but there was a great gulf fixed between the two, and he couldn't pass over.

And in hell he lift up his eyes . . . (Luke 16:23). That really means the place of departed spirits of the wicked dead. These were in torment.

Jesus made His grave there. Nobody made Him go. He went by choice to receive the wages of sin on your behalf.

If there's any part of hell Jesus did not suffer, you'll have to suffer it. But, thank God, Jesus suffered it *all*, for **you!**

In the place of the wicked dead, all the demons of hell and Satan rejoiced over the prize. The corridors of hell were filled with joy. "We've done it! We've captured the Son of God! We'll no longer be in the pit of the damned! The earth and all that is therein is ours! Forever it will be ours!" Rejoicing in hell had never been so great as it was that day. But it was short-lived.

Jesus Crossed the Gulf

Jesus stayed in hell long enough to satisfy justice. Then He was raised for our justification.

When Jesus was in the pit of hell, in that terrible torment, no doubt the Devil and his emissaries gathered around to see the annihilation of God's Son. But in the corridors of hell, there came a great voice from heaven: **"Turn Him loose! He's there illegally!"** And all of hell became paralyzed.

I imagine the footsteps of Jesus were heard echoing through those corridors. "Shut the gates!" the evil ones cried.

"Don't let Him out or He will ascend to the throne!"

But Jesus, the Son of God, arose—born again of the Spirit of God. He walked over to Satan and stripped from him the keys of death, hell, and the grave, and tore the gates off their hinges!

Then He crossed the gulf to the place of the righteous dead and preached to them, saying, "There's no need for you to stay here. Your resurrection has come!" He led captivity captive.

Some of those righteous dead were seen in the streets of Jerusalem. Don't you know that jerked the slack out of those Sadducees! They had said there was no resurrection of the dead. (Someone suggested that's why they were *sad-you-see!*) But it was hard to perpetrate their doctrine with Uncle Jack walking down the street when he had been dead for twenty-nine years!

Paul said in Colossians 2:15, *And having spoiled principalities and powers, he made a shew of them openly, triumphing over them in it.* The word *spoiled* literally means "stripped off or unclothed."

Satan doesn't have a thing to wear. His authority is gone.

Jesus Stripped Satan of His Authority

The Apostle Paul said, *There is no power but of God: the powers that be are ordained of God* (Rom. 13:1). The reason the evil ones have no power is because Jesus stripped them. They no longer have *any* authority in the earth, unless *you* give them *your* authority.

Allow me to paraphrase what Isaiah, the prophet, said: "They will look upon Satan in the Millennium and say, 'You mean that is the thing that deceived the world? *That little thing?* You mean I let that thing run over me?'"

The judgment of this world has already come. The crisis is past. **The prince of this world has been cast out!**

11
Jesus, The Sin Offering

I realize that many of the statements I have made in this book could only be called theory without Old Testament types to bear them out. So we will begin with the Book of Leviticus, chapter 6.

. . . The Lord spake unto Moses, saying, Speak unto Aaron and to his sons, saying, This is the law of the sin offering: In the place where the burnt offering is killed shall the sin offering be killed before the Lord: it is most holy. The priest that offereth it for sin shall eat it: in the holy place shall it be eaten, in the court of the tabernacle of the congregation (Lev. 6:24-26).

At first glance, it sounds like the high priest is going to eat the sacrifice. But notice verse 30: *And no sin offering, whereof any of the blood is brought into the tabernacle of the congregation to reconcile withal in the holy place, shall be eaten: it shall be burnt in the fire.*

Sin Offering Burnt

Jesus was the Sin Offering. The Sin Offering shall be burnt in the fire. The Psalmist David tapped into it: . . . *Thou hast delivered my soul from the lowest hell* (Ps. 86:13). These prophetic words refer to Jesus being delivered from hell.

Listen to the words of Jesus. *For as Jonas was three days and three nights in the whale's belly so shall the Son of man be three days and three nights in the heart of the earth* (Matt. 12:40).

In the heart of the earth. In the *center* of the earth, *not* in the *grave*. That's where hell is—in the center of the earth. There are several places in the Scriptures that indicate this.

Whatsoever shall touch the flesh thereof shall be holy: and when there is sprinkled of the blood thereof upon any garment, thou shalt wash that whereon it was sprinkled in the holy place.

But the earthen vessel wherein it is sodden **shall be broken:** *and if it be sodden in a brasen pot, it shall be both scoured, and rinsed in water. All the males among the priests shall eat thereof: it is most holy.*

And no sin offering, whereof any of the blood is brought into the tabernacle of the congregation to reconcile withal in the holy place, shall be eaten: it shall be burnt in the fire.

Leviticus 6:27-30

In other words, the Sin Offering (that represents Jesus) could not be eaten. It had to be burned.

I want you to notice verse 28. *The earthen vessel wherein it is sodden shall be broken.* Listen to the prophetic words concerning Jesus. *I am forgotten as a dead man out of mind: I am like a broken vessel* (Ps. 31:12).

The First Death

Isaiah said, "He made His grave with the wicked . . . in His *deaths.*" As He hung on the cross, Jesus—the Lamb, the unblemished Sin Offering, the Son of God—remained holy until the last breath left His body.

When He breathed His last breath, He said, *It is finished.* He gave Himself up to physical death and then received spiritual death, *after* the Sin Offering was made.

I want you to see the Old Testament type: **how He delivered Himself to death and received sin.** Notice Leviticus

16:5: *And he shall take of the congregation of the children of Israel two kids of the goats for a sin offering, and one ram for a burnt offering.* Now the burnt offering was for Aaron, the priest who offered it.

And he shall take the two goats, and present them before the Lord at the door of the tabernacle of the congregation. And Aaron shall cast lots upon the two goats; one lot for the Lord, and the other lot for the scapegoat.

And Aaron shall bring the goat upon which the Lord's lot fell, and offer him for a sin offering. But the goat on which the lot fell to be the scapegoat, shall be presented alive before the Lord (vv. 7-10).

These two goats represent Jesus. You can't use just one; there must be two. One was for the sin offering; the other was to receive the judgment (punishment) or the just recompense due sin. **The two goats made one complete sacrifice.**

The Second Death

Now the Sin Offering is killed. Jesus, on the cross, gave Himself up to physical death for a Sin Offering. There was *no* sin in Him. That's the reason He qualifies. He is unblemished, and that Offering is *most holy*.

But once the Sin Offering was accomplished, His Spirit must be presented before God to receive the just recompense of reward. *The soul that sinneth, it shall die.* No! **Jesus didn't sin, but man did!** *The wages of sin is death* (Rom. 6:23).

And death and hell were cast into the lake of fire. This is the second death. And whosoever was not found written in the book of life was cast into the lake of fire (Rev. 20:14,15).

The Bible is plain: The wage must be received. Justice must be carried out. To obtain eternal redemption, an eternal price must be paid. Physical life is not eternal.

Remember Jesus' words, *Father, into thy hands I commend my Spirit . . .* (Luke 24:46). If God's going to redeem us from the second death, someone *must pay* that penalty. The second death is spiritual. It is separation from God.

This is something that is awesome, yet I am convinced the Scriptures reveal that Jesus became spiritually *dead* in order to obtain spiritual *life* for us! You can make up your own mind as we look at these Old Testament types.

The Sin Offering

Now follow this closely:

Then shall he kill the goat of the sin offering that is for the people, and bring his blood within the veil, and do with that blood as he did with the blood of the bullock, and sprinkle it upon the mercy seat, and before the mercy seat:

And he shall make an atonement for the holy place, because of the uncleanness of the children of Israel, and because of their trangressions in all their sins.

Leviticus 16:15,16

This is a type or foreshadowing of the blood of Jesus making atonement for the sins of the world.

. . . and so shall he do for the tabernacle of the congregation, that remaineth among them in the midst of their uncleanness . . . And when he hath made an end of reconciling the holy place, and the tabernacle of the congregation, and the altar, he shall bring the live goat (vv. 16,20).

Notice it is the *holy place* atoned for *after* an offering for the sins of the people has been made. Then they bring

the other goat. The second goat is a type
of Jesus after He expired, having
already made the decision to open His
Spirit to God to do what was necessary
to satisfy the claims of justice and to
redeem the world. Eternal redemption
was at stake.

Jesus, The Scapegoat

*And Aaron shall lay both his hands
upon the head of the live goat, and confess
over him all the iniquities of the children of
Israel, and all their transgressions in all
their sins, putting them upon the head of the
goat* (v. 21).

Someone has suggested that sin is
personal disobedience and that sin
could not be put on anyone. But we
read in Isaiah that God put our
iniquities on Jesus. We find it here in
the Old Testament type that the high
priest who offered the sacrifice laid his
hands—not *one*, but *both*—upon the *head*
of the goat.

Jesus is the *Head* of the Church. *Who*
offered Jesus as sacrifice for the world?
God. Abraham prophesied, "God will
provide Himself a Lamb." *God* is the
One Who offered the sacrifice. He was

the High Priest Who laid His hands on the Head of the goat.

Then, according to this type, it would be God Who laid *his hands* upon the eternal Spirit of Jesus and confessed on Him the iniquities of all the people.

. . . and all their transgressions in all their sins, putting them upon the head of the goat, and shall send him away by the hand of a fit man into the wilderness: and the goat shall bear upon him all their iniquities unto a land not inhabited (vv. 21,22).

(*Webster's New 20th Century Dictionary* says *death* in theology means separation of the soul from God; also, a being under the dominion of sin, destitute of grace or divine life, called *spiritual death*.)

If you have a center column reference, there is a note that says the Hebrew words *not inhabited* in verse 22 mean "separation." So the goat was sent to a *land of separation.* **Spiritual death means separation from God.**

The first goat is already dead. The physical death has already taken place. But this is the *second* death. This is the *plural death* that Isaiah prophesied.

The second goat did not cease to exist. He was sent to a land of separation. This is the type of spiritual death. When Adam died spiritually, his spirit did not cease to exist.

Satan is a spirit. He is spiritually dead, but he still exists. Spirits are eternal. They never cease to exist. For the second goat to be a true type, it had to exist to receive the judgment of justice.

After the blood of Jesus was spilled to atone the Holy Place, the veil was rent from top to bottom. The Sin Offering had been made. The Holy Place was atoned. The way to the Holy of Holies was opened, but judgment had to be done. The sins and iniquities had to be carried away. Then *Jesus* became sin and *carried it away* to an uninhabitable place, a place of separation.

One translation says, ". . . a place not fit for human habitation." Hell was created for the Devil and his angels, not for man. God never intended for man to go there. Jesus bore sin into the pit of hell. **He carried it into the region of the damned to do away with sin!**

The goat shall bear upon him all their iniquities unto a land not inhabited: and he shall let go the goat in the wilderness. And Aaron shall come into the tabernacle of the congregation, and shall put off the linen garments, which he put on when he went into the holy place, and shall leave them there.

And he shall wash his flesh with water in the holy place, and put on his garments, and come forth, and offer his burnt offering, and the burnt offering of the people, and make an atonement for himself, and for the people.

And the fat of the sin offering shall he burn upon the altar. And he that let go the goat for the scapegoat shall wash his clothes, and bathe his flesh in water, and afterward come into the camp (vv. 22-26).

Holy Sin Offering

Some have stated that Jesus did not really become sin because the Sin Offering remained holy. But notice that *one* goat was *holy* (Sin Offering); *the other* goat was *contaminated* with the sins of others—not the sins of His own, but the *sins of others*.

The Sin Offering remained holy. It could not be contaminated. Everything that touched it was made holy. The Sin Offering being already offered, the scapegoat is brought before the High Priest (God). He laid both hands upon the scapegoat and confessed all the sins of the people upon the second goat.

Now let's look again at the type. The human spirit of Jesus is as the scapegoat. The spirit of Jesus is eternal. He is to obtain eternal redemption. The high priest who offered the sacrifice laid his hand upon the head of the goat. God is the High Priest Who offered Jesus.

The last words Jesus said before He died were, *Father, into thy hands I commend my spirit* (Luke 23:46). *Type:* God (High Priest) laid His hands upon His Son Jesus and confessed the sins, iniquities, and transgressions of the people, putting them upon Him (Jesus).

The goat was so contaminated that the person who let it go into the wilderness is considered contaminated and must bathe and wash his clothes before getting back into the holy place.

The first goat was holy. The second was contaminated with the sins of others.

But anyone who was touched by the flesh or blood of the Sin Offering was called *holy*. The Church has never seen what God did to redeem man. He made the spirit of His Son to be sin. He bore that sin burden of the world.

No doubt, that's what brought the drops of blood from His veins as He knelt in the Garden of Gethsemane. He wasn't afraid of physical death. **It was the separation of that second death that He dreaded.**

And the bullock for the sin offering, and the goat for the sin offering, whose blood was brought in to make atonement in the holy place, shall one carry forth without the camp; and they shall burn in the fire their skins, and their flesh, and their dung.

And he that burneth them shall wash his clothes, and bathe his flesh in water, and afterward he shall come into the camp (vv. 27,28).

Prophetic Words of Revelation

The prophetic word of Isaiah and others reveal hidden truths that man did not see. Job tapped into prophecy concerning Jesus' suffering that has gone practically unnoticed. Many of the prophets would drift in and out of prophecy as David did on many occasions.

The whole 29th chapter of Job is no doubt Jesus speaking in His suffering; it won't fit anyone but *Jesus.*

Notice verses 12-18:

Because I delivered the poor that cried, and the fatherless, and him that had none to help him. The blessing of him that was ready to perish came upon me: and I caused the widow's heart to sing for joy.

I put on righteousness, and it clothed me: my judgment was as a robe and a diadem. I was eyes to the blind, and feet was I to the lame. I was a father to the poor: and the cause which I knew not I searched out.

And I brake the jaws of the wicked, and plucked the spoil out of his teeth. Then I said, I shall die in my nest, and I shall multiply my days as the sand.

Then in Job, chapter 30, there is prophecy:

They abhor me, they flee far from me, and spare not to spit in my face . . .

Terrors are turned upon me: they pursue my soul as the wind: and my welfare passeth away as a cloud.

And now my soul is poured out upon me; the days of affliction have taken hold upon me. My bones are pierced in me in the night season: and my sinews take no rest. By the great force of my disease is my garment changed: it bindeth me about as the collar of my coat.

He hath cast me into the mire, and I am become like dust and ashes. I cry unto thee, and thou dost not hear me: I stand up, and thou regardest me not. Thou art become cruel to me: with thy strong hand thou opposest thyself against me.

Thou liftest me up to the wind; thou causest me to ride upon it, and dissolvest my substance. For I know that thou wilt bring me to death, and to the house appointed for all living.

Howbeit he will not stretch out his hand to the grave, though they cry in his destruction. Did not I weep for him that was in trouble? was not my soul grieved for the poor? When I looked for good, then evil came unto me: and when I waited for light, there came darkness.

My bowels boiled, and rested not: the days of affliction prevented me. I went mourning without the sun: I stood up, and I cried in the congregation. I am a brother to dragons, and a companion to owls. My skin is black upon me, and **my bones are burned with heat** *(vv. 10,15-30).*

For my soul is full of troubles: and my life draweth nigh unto the grave. **I am counted with them that go down into the pit:** *I am as a man that hath no strength: Free among the dead, like the slain that lie in the grave, whom thou rememberest no more: and they are cut off from thy hand.*

Thou hast laid me in the lowest pit, in darkness, in the deeps. Thy wrath lieth hard upon me, and thou hast afflicted me with all thy waves. Selah. Thou hast put away mine acquaintance far from me; thou hast made me an abomination unto them: I am shut up, and I cannot come forth.

I am afflicted and ready to die from my youth up: while I suffer thy terrors I am distracted. Thy fierce wrath goeth over me; thy terrors have cut me off.

Psalm 88:3-8,15,16

Then the prophet Isaiah said, *He was taken from prison and from judgment: and who shall declare his generation? for he was cut off out of the land of the living: for the transgression of my people was he stricken* (Is. 53:8).

Eternal Redemption

Eternal redemption was at stake. *For it is not possible that the blood of bulls and of goats should take away sins. Wherefore when he cometh into the world, he saith Sacrifice and offering thou wouldest not, but a body hast thou prepared me: in burnt offerings and sacrifices for sin thou hast had no pleasure* (Heb. 10:4-6).

Jesus became the Sin Offering, but it took more than that to give man eternal redemption!

Then said I, Lo, I come (in the volume of the book it is written of me,) to do thy will O God. Above when he said, Sacrifice and offering and burnt offerings and offering for sin thou wouldest not, neither hadst pleasure therein; which are offered by the law;

Then said he, Lo, I come to do thy will, O God. He taketh away the first, that he may establish the second. By the which will we are sanctified through the offering of the body of Jesus Christ once for all (vv. 7-10).

But this man, after he had offered one sacrifice for sins for ever, sat down on the right hand of God; from henceforth expecting till his enemies he made his footstool (vv. 12,13).

One Complete Sacrifice

The two goats are considered one complete sacrifice. Without the scapegoat, it couldn't be complete because it wouldn't have been carried away. Judgment will fall where Jesus carried those sins (hell).

The Old Testament offering just simply swept the sins under the rug, covered them up where they couldn't see them. This was not going to cover, but bring *eternal redemption.* Man would have no more consciousness of sin.

Jesus bore that sin upon Himself. Paul saw it. *For he hath made him to be sin for us . . .* (2 Cor. 5:21). God made Him to be sin. Jesus didn't sin. He *became* sin. He gladly swallowed up sin and carried it to the unihabitable place.

The *sin* problem is cured! *Jesus Christ of Nazareth bore it away!* We still have a *sinner* problem, but Jesus is also the cure for the sinner problem.

For by one offering he hath perfected for ever them that are sanctified . . . This is the covenant that I will make with them after those days, saith the Lord, I will put my laws into their hearts, and in their minds will I write them (vv. 14,16). (It is a spiritual law He's talking about writing in their hearts.)

And their sins and iniquities will I remember no more. Now where remission of these is, there is no more offering for sin. Having therefore, brethren, boldness to enter into the holiest by the blood of Jesus, by a new and living way, which he hath consecrated for us, through the veil, that is to say, his flesh (the Sin Offering) . . . (vv. 17-20).

Let's go back to Hebrews 9:8. *The Holy Ghost this signifying, that the way into the holiest of all was not yet made manifest, while as the first tabernacle was yet standing.*

Neither by the blood of goats and calves, but by his own blood he entered in once into the holy place, having obtained eternal redemption for us (v. 12). Eternal redemption is ours! He didn't enter in there until He had *obtained* eternal redemption for us!

You remember when He appeared to Mary at the tomb? He said, "Don't touch Me, for I have not yet ascended to My Father." He had to ascend to heaven and sprinkle His blood upon the mercy seat.

The next time He appeared to the disciples He told Thomas, "Touch Me, handle Me." He had *already* entered in and obtained eternal redemption for us.

Eternal Sacrifice

*For if the blood of bulls and of goats, and the ashes of an heifer sprinkling the unclean, sanctifieth to the purifying of the flesh: how much **more** shall the blood of Christ, **who through the eternal Spirit** offered himself without spot to God . . .* (Heb. 9:13,14).

How was it done? **Through the eternal spirit within Him.** He opened His eternal spirit to God once He expired. His last words were, *Father, into thy hands I commend my spirit* (Luke 23:46).

In the Old Testament types, the priest that offered the sacrifices (which could be no one but God, for only God could touch His Spirit) laid his hands upon the head of the goat (or upon the eternal spirit). Notice, the first goat is dead; the Sin Offering has already been made. Then it was sent away into an uninhabited place so judgment would fall out there upon it and not come on the people.

How much more shall the blood of Christ, who through the eternal Spirit offered himself without spot to God, purge your conscience from dead works to serve the living God? And for this cause he is the mediator of the new testament, that by means of death, for the redemption of the transgressions that were under the first testament, they which are called might receive the promise of eternal inheritance (Heb. 9:14,15).

Eternal redemption requires an eternal sacrifice. It had to be a *complete* sacrifice. It had to be a *total* commitment. That's why Jesus sweat drops of blood in the Garden, for where the testament is, there must be of necessity the death of the testator.

Death of Testator

To obtain eternal redemption, the eternal spirit had to bear away sin to a place of judgment. **This was the second death.** Jesus died spiritually, not for any of His own sin! He became the serpent on the pole, the snake on the ground, in the Old Testament type. He did this so that He might swallow up evil and carry it away where judgment would fall there in hell and not upon those who received the redemption. That ought to get the whole world born again! And I'm convinced it would, if the world knew about it!

A testament is a force after men are dead; it is of no strength at all while the testator lives. There is no doubt about it: To obtain eternal redemption, an eternal spirit had to be sacrificed. There is one point I want to make clear. Jesus' spirit did not cease to exist. Spirits *never* cease to exist. Jesus' spirit became spiritually dead.

Adam died spiritually when he ate of the fruit. Jesus died spiritually when He opened Himself to sin. He allowed it to come. God put it upon Him. The Holy Son of God didn't sin! He *became* sin for you and me. He became a spiritually dead man. He was separated from His Father God—a spiritual separation—and the prophet Isaiah saw it. He saw two deaths: physical, then spiritual.

"The reason the Son of God was made manifest (visible) was to undo (destroy, loosen and dissolve) the works the devil [has done]" (1 John 3:8 AMP).

Jesus came to undo what Satan had done. Adam committed sin and died spiritually. Adam's spiritual death produced physical death. *For the wages of sin is death.*

See this contrast: Jesus became obedient to a physical death which was not due Him. *He made the decision before He died to bear the iniquities of the world.* Also, He bore the *full* penalty for those sins, which was spiritual death or separation from God, to restore man to fellowship with God.

Jesus made the decision to *die* while He was alive.

Men today must make the decision to *live* before they die!

Jesus reversed the process: Adam died spiritually, *then* physically. Jesus died physically, *then* spiritually. As the wage of sin is death, so is the gift of righteousness, *eternal life.*

Let's take a look at the way the Spirit of God spoke through the Apostle Paul in Romans 5:12,14-19:

Wherefore, as by one man sin entered into the world, and death by sin; and so death passed upon all men, for that all have sinned . . . Nevertheless death reigned from Adam to Moses, even over them that had not sinned after the similitude of Adam's transgression, who is the figure of him that was to come.

But not as the offence, so also is the free gift. For if through the offence of one many be dead, much more the grace of God, and the gift by grace, which is by one man, Jesus Christ, hath abounded unto many.

And not as it was by one that sinned, so is the gift: for the judgment was by one to condemnation, but the free gift is of many offences unto justification.

For if by one man's offence death reigned by one; much more they which receive abundance of grace and of the gift of righteousness shall reign in life by one, Jesus Christ.

Therefore as by the offence of one judgment came upon all men to condemnation; even so by the righteousness of one the free gift came upon all men unto justification of life.

For as by one man's disobedience many were made sinners, so by the obedience of one shall many be made righteous.

Yes, Jesus obtained eternal redemption for us!

12
Jesus, A Type of the Rod

There are many truths hidden in the Scriptures. But we don't want to build a thought on just *one* scripture. *In the mouth of two or three witnesses shall every word be established* (2 Cor. 13:1).

You can find a type of Jesus in every book in the Bible. Even beginning with Genesis, we get some previews of what God is about to do in the earth to redeem mankind from a life of destruction. Some of the greatest truths in the Bible are found in the Old Testament types.

There have been many Old Testament types that you've wondered, *"How* could it be? *Why* did God set forth these types?" As we look into the Word, we will see what God had in mind as He began to shape the destiny of man by these Old Testament types.

And there shall come forth a rod out of the stem of Jesse, and a Branch shall grow out of his roots:

And the spirit of the Lord shall rest upon him, the spirit of wisdom and understanding, the spirit of counsel and might, the spirit of knowledge and of the fear of the Lord;

And shall make him of quick understanding in the fear of the Lord: and he shall not judge after the sight of his eyes, neither reprove after the hearing of his ears:

But with righteousness shall he judge the poor, and reprove with equity for the meek of the earth: and he shall smite the earth with the rod of his mouth, and with the breath of his lips shall he slay the wicked.

And righteousness shall be the girdle of his loins, and faithfulness the girdle of his reins.

Isaiah 11:1-5

The thing I want you to notice is the word *rod*. Jesus is called the Rod *out of the stem of Jesse*. He talks about God smiting the earth with the Rod of His mouth. Jesus was the Word of God; the Word spoken out of His mouth is what He is talking about. *Jesus* and *the Word* are one and the Rod is representative of Jesus.

With this in mind, let's go to Exodus, chapter 7, and look at an Old Testament type of Jesus taking sin and doing away with it. You know the story of Pharaoh. Moses and Aaron have gone before him and said, "Let our people go."

In verse 9, God is speaking: *When Pharaoh shall speak unto you, saying, Shew a miracle for you: then thou shalt say unto Aaron, Take thy rod, and cast it before Pharaoh, and it shall become a serpent.*

And Moses and Aaron went in unto Pharaoh, and they did so as the Lord had commanded: and Aaron cast down his rod before Pharaoh (v. 10).

Now remember, the rod is a type of Jesus. When Aaron cast down the rod before Pharaoh, it turned into a serpent, which is representative of sin or evil. God has given Pharaoh, and the Devil, a preview of what's about to happen in the earth. But Satan isn't smart enough to figure it out; neither is Pharaoh.

Pharaoh said, "That's nothing. Call my magicians!"

When Pharoah's magicians cast down their rods, they turned into serpents also. But Aaron's rod swallowed up their serpents. Aaron's rod turned into a *king* snake, and king snakes eat other snakes.

Now, here's a type of Jesus becoming sin. **He became sin that He might swallow up sin!** This is one of the Old Testament types of Jesus dying spiritually and becoming sin for the purpose of doing away with sin!

This begins to show the plan of God before Pharaoh, the Devil, and the world. It was a preview of what was about to take place.

But they can't figure out what in the world is going on. What's all this snake business, anyway? The rod (the type of Jesus) becomes a serpent. He became sin so that He might swallow up sin and do away with sin! Because the rod swallowed up *all* the other serpents, sin is defeated!

Let's go to another Old Testament type in the Book of Numbers, chapter 14. You find the children of Israel complaining. God said to Moses and Aaron, *Say unto them, As truly as I live, saith the Lord, as ye have spoken in mine ears, so will I do to you* (v. 28).

We read in Numbers 21:5, after God told the people they would have what they said, *The people spake against God, and against Moses, Wherefore have ye brought us up out of Egypt to die in the wilderness?*

And God had just told Moses to tell them, "I'm going to do exactly what they say," and they said, "We are going to die in the wilderness."

And the Lord sent fiery serpents among the people, and they bit the people; and much people of Israel died (v. 6).

God told the people what was going to happen. His Word was out, and God cannot lie. It was *an allowing sense*. God had to allow it to come; if He had stopped it, He would have violated His Word.

Therefore the people came to Moses, and said, We have sinned, for we have spoken against the Lord, and against thee; pray unto the Lord, that he take away the serpents from us. And Moses prayed for the people.

And the Lord said unto Moses, Make thee a fiery serpent, and set it upon a pole:

*and it shall come to pass that every one that
is bitten, when he looketh upon it, shall live*
(vv. 7,8).

Who is that serpent He put upon the
pole? **Jesus, the Healer!** Today medical
doctors use the symbol of a serpent on a
pole as a symbol of healing. That ought
to tell us something. **Jesus bore your
sicknesses to bring healing to you.**

For years I couldn't understand why
in the world God told Moses to put a
serpent on that pole. I thought He had
made a mistake; He should have put a
little lamb on the pole. Jesus was the
Lamb of God, slain from the foundation
of the world.

The pole is symbolic of the cross—a
place of execution. The serpent on the
pole is symbolic of Jesus becoming sin
after the Sin Offering was made. It is
also symbolic of divine judgment upon
that old serpent, Satan.

As Moses lifted up the serpent in the
wilderness, even so must the Son of
Man be lifted up. As Jesus said to His
disciples, *And I, if I be lifted up from the
earth, will draw all men unto me* (John
12:32).

Jesus willingly gave Himself to the cross and to death. He became the Sin Offering. Once the Sin Offering was received, God made Him (Jesus) to become sin for us. He, Who knew no sin, became sin. *The sinless son of God became as a serpent that He might swallow up all evil.*

Jesus dealt a death blow to Satan on the cross. They *both* died in the same battle. Divine judgment rendered Satan harmless and ineffective against the new creation that was to come by Jesus' victorious resurrection.

If you will behold what happened when the sin offering was made and the fact that Jesus became a serpent upon the pole, it will change your life. Satan, that old serpent, cannot afflict you in any manner. If you will behold what happened on the cross, *you will live also*! The law of the Spirit of life in Christ Jesus has made you *free* from the law of sin and death.

A Symbol of Divine Judgment

Brass is symbolic of divine judgment. A brass serpent can't hurt you because it has no life. That is what

Jesus came to do: ... *For this purpose was the Son of God manifested that he might destroy the works of the devil.*

There it is again: the Old Testament type of Jesus on the cross. He became a serpent of brass on a pole.

... and it came to pass that if a serpent had bitten any man, when he beheld the serpent of brass, he lived (Num. 21:9).

Jesus said, *As Moses lifted up the serpent in the wilderness, even so must the Son of man be lifted up* (John 3:14).

The serpent on the pole has a twofold meaning. It is what we would call *the law of double reference.* Jesus became the serpent, but the brass is symbolic of divine judgment. Divine judgment was poured out upon Jesus to destroy the power of the serpent. Since that has taken place, the serpent is powerless. Jesus destroyed his ability; his power is gone. Jesus spoiled principalities and powers; He made a show of them openly, triumphing over them in it. (Col. 2:15.)

Jesus, the Son of God, *paralyzed* Satan!

No one is afraid of a brass serpent because it is harmless. A brass snake can't bite anyone. Satan has been paralyzed by the death-dealing blow of Jesus. The seed of the woman bruised his head. Divine judgment rendered that old serpent harmless and ineffective. If you will behold what Jesus did, you will see that old serpent, the Devil, as a brass serpent, rendered harmless by divine judgment.

The Bible said Jesus paralyzed him. We find in Hebrews 2:14 these words: *Forasmuch then as the children are partakers of flesh and blood, he also himself likewise took part of the same; that through death he might **destroy** him that had the power of death, that is, the devil.*

The word translated *destroy* should be *paralyzed*. He *paralyzed* him who had the power of death, that is, the Devil.

And deliver them who through fear of death were all their lifetime subject to bondage (v. 15).

Jesus delivered us from the fear of the death-dealing blow of Satan. We don't have to fear that brass serpent. He has been rendered harmless and ineffective by divine judgment.

Joseph, A Type of Jesus

Joseph is an Old Testament type of Jesus. Even though his own family didn't believe in him, in the end they bowed to him.

God gave Joseph revelation of things to come, but his family didn't receive it. His brothers cast him in a well and sold him into slavery in Egypt. (Gen. 37:28.) Jesus came to earth saying what His Father said, but His own people cast Him. out. God put our iniquities on Him. (Is. 53:6.)

Joseph ascended from the bottom of a well to a place of authority because of God's Word to him. His name was known through all Egypt. Jesus ascended from the pit of the damned to the right hand of the Father, far above all principalities and powers. "His name is above every name." (Phil. 2:9.)

Joseph bought all the land in time of famine. (Gen. 47:20.) Jesus purchased all the world with His blood. (John 3:16.)

The brothers of Joseph delivered him up for evil, but God turned it for good to save all who would come to Him. (Gen. 50:20.) Jesus was delivered up to death by evil men, but God used it *to save all who would come to him.* (1 Cor. 2:7,8; Rom. 5:17.)

Joseph was punished for things he did not do. (Gen. 39:20.) **Jesus took punishment that belonged to us.** (Is. 53:5,6.)

Joseph became a slave that he might make Israel rich. (Gen. 37:28.) Jesus became poor so that *you* might be rich. (2 Cor. 8:9.)

All of Egypt bowed before Joseph. Egypt is a type of the world and sin. **All sin bowed to Jesus.**

13
First-Begotten of the Dead

Why do the heathen rage, and the people imagine a vain thing? The kings of the earth set themselves, and the rulers take counsel together, against the Lord, and against his anointed, saying, **Let us break their bands asunder, and cast away their cords from us.**

Then shall he speak unto them in his wrath, and vex them in his sore displeasure. Yet have I set my king upon my holy hill of Zion. I will declare the decree: the Lord hath said unto me, Thou art my Son; this day have I begotten thee.

Psalm 2:1-3,5-7

What is He talking about when He says, . . . *This day have I begotten thee*? Is He talking about when Jesus was born in a manger? We find the answer in Acts 13:30-34:

But God raised him from the dead; and he was seen many days of them which came

*up with him from Galilee to Jerusalem, who
are his witnesses unto the people.*

*And we declare unto you glad tidings,
how that the promise which was made unto
the fathers, God hath fulfilled the same unto
us their children, in that he **hath raised up
Jesus again;** as it is also written in the
second psalm, Thou art my Son, this day
have I begotten thee. And **as concerning
that he raised him up from the dead,** now
no more to return to corruption, he said on
this wise, I will give you the sure mercies of
David.*

That is when God said it—when He
raised Jesus from the dead. . . . *this day
have I begotten thee.*

What is He talking about? To find
the answer, let's go to Hebrews 1:4,5.
*Being made so much better than the angels,
as he hath by inheritance obtained a more
excellent name than they. For unto which of
the angels said he at any time, Thou art my
Son, **this day have I begotten thee** . . . .*
You will notice that God didn't say that
to any of the *angels.* God said that to
Jesus the day He raised Him from the
dead. . . . *And again, I will be to him a
Father, and he shall be to me a Son.*

He begins to unfold a hidden mystery of God's redemptive plan, which is almost unknown to the Church today. Because Jesus became sin and separated Himself from God, God must be a Father to Him *once again*.

But one in a certain place testified, saying, What is man, that thou art mindful of him? or the Son of man that thou visitest him? Thou madest him a little lower than the angels; then crownedst him with glory and honour, and didst set him over the works of thy hands:

Thou hast put all things in subjection under his feet. For in that he put all in subjection under him, he left nothing that is not put under him.

But now we see not yet all things put under him. But we see Jesus, who was made a little lower than the angels for the suffering of death, crowned with glory and honour; that he by the grace of God should taste death for every man.

Hebrews 2:6-9

Notice **Jesus tasted death for every man.** What *kind* of death is Paul talking about? It must be **spiritual** death. If Paul were speaking of *physical* death, *then no one would ever have to die physically.*

Because of Jesus' suffering spiritual separation, the sinner can be redeemed from spiritual death. (You realize Paul is not speaking of physical death here.) Never again will there *have to be* spiritual death. You *can* die spiritually, but you don't *have* to. **It will be an act of your will if you do.** Jesus died for the sinner. He tasted death so that the sinner could be redeemed.

The sinner is not going to heaven just because Jesus died for him. **He has to be born again.** He is a child of the Devil. But Jesus has already swallowed up that punishment and man's sins are forgiven. If the sinner will believe and confess Jesus as his Lord, he will have a new lease on *life!*

For both he that sanctifieth and they who are sanctified are all of one: for which cause he is not ashamed to call them brethren, saying, I will declare thy name unto my brethren, in the midst of the church will I sing praise unto thee.

And again, I will put my trust in him. And again, Behold I and the children which God hath given me. Forasmuch then as the children are partakers of flesh and blood, he also himself likewise took part of the same;

that through death he might destroy him (or paralyze him) *that had the power of death, that is, the devil.*

Hebrews 2:11-14

So also Christ glorified not himself to be made an high priest; but he that said unto him, Thou art my Son, to day have I begotten thee.

Hebrews 5:5

As we look at the scriptural reference concerning Jesus' dying for us spiritually, I want you to notice it isn't something somebody has just thought up. It is Bible truth, not theory. It will release you into a greater area of faith and understanding as you know what Jesus did to bring about your salvation.

To *fully appreciate* what Jesus did for us, we need to know He went to hell, received punishment *for our sins*, and obtained *eternal redemption* for us.

You cannot receive eternal redemption by physical sacrifices. That's the reason the old law wouldn't work, why the old law wouldn't redeem man from sin consciousness.

Firstborn Among Many

For whom he did foreknow, he also did predestinate to be conformed to the image of his Son, that he might be the firstborn among many brethren.

Romans 8:29

Jesus is the firstborn among many brethren. Paul can't be referring to Jesus being the first to be raised from the dead; Lazarus and others were raised to life again. He is talking about the first to be born from spiritual death to spiritual life.

For whom he did foreknow, he also did predestinate . . . . He foreknew Jesus. Jesus was with Him from the beginning.

Now don't read something into this that He didn't say. There is a twofold meaning here. He isn't saying that people are predestined either to be saved or not saved. He is saying that everyone who receives Jesus is *born again* and will be poured out of the same mold that Jesus was when He became the firstborn among many brethren.

When Jesus was raised from the dead, He was born again of the Spirit of God. Jesus said to Nicodemus, *That which is born of the flesh is flesh; and that which is born of the Spirit is spirit.*

We just read in Romans 8:29 where Jesus was called *the firstborn among many brethren.* In other words, there isn't going to be one born from spiritual death to life, but *many* born just as He was!

That was bad news to Satan. Satan had his hands full with Jesus here on this earth. Satan was making folks sick, and Jesus was healing them. Satan killed Lazarus with sickness; Jesus came along, raised him from the dead, and healed him.

Satan thought, *If I can just get rid of Jesus, I will have it made.* He thought he had succeeded in getting rid of Jesus, but he found out he couldn't hold Him in hell. **Jesus was born again before his eyes!** He became *the firstborn among many brethren!* In other words, there are going to be millions and millions of them *exactly like Jesus!*

On the day of Pentecost in the upper room, 120 were born again, just like Jesus. Then, before the day was over, *3,000 more* were born again. That's bad news for Satan: *3,120 born again—***just like Jesus.**

We find in the Bible that Jesus is called "the only begotten Son" *until the day He was raised from the dead.* Then in every reference to Jesus after that, as pertaining to the time *after* His resurrection, **He is *never* called "the only begotten."** On occasions they refer back to Him as "the only begotten," *before* He was raised from the dead, but they're *not* referring to the present time.

In Genesis 22:16,17 God said to Abraham, *Because thou hast done this thing . . . thy seed shall possess the gate of his enemies.* Let me remind you that Jesus said to Peter, "I will build My Church, and the gates of hell shall not prevail against it."

Jesus said, "I'm going to build *My Church*!" Man has tried to build it all these years, but has failed. Jesus said, "I'll build My Church."

God is in the process, through Jesus Christ of Nazareth, of building the Church today! You're going to see the *greatest* Church the world has ever known.

A Prophetic Utterance

As I was teaching on this in one of my meetings, the spirit of prophecy came on me and this prophetic word came forth:

"For the day is at hand when the ministry of the Word of God shall come alive in the Church. Those who have been dead to the things of God shall *rise to their feet* and *walk in the wisdom and in the power of God!*

"*The strength of Almighty God shall flow in the midst of them!* So shall they walk in the avenue of life until the wisdom that flows from their lips shall astound the world.

"For they'll speak of the Spirit of God. The anointing of God will arise within them. The angels and ministering spirits shall become very much involved in the lives of the believers who will stand to their feet in this day and *walk* in the principles of the Word.

"So shall the anointing of God flow in the earth. And so shall the Church of Almighty God be built! It will come as an explosion, as it were, by the power of the Spirit of God.

"And so shall they rise here and rise there. They'll rise from obscurity. You will see churches rising from one to three thousand in three months' time.

"You will see the *mighty anointing of God* work in the earth. You shall see the restoration of the children of God. They shall be restored to their rightful place, and the power of *the Living Christ* shall be shed abroad throughout the land. You'll see it in your generation.

"Because, you see, there are people who have turned themselves from the Word and are preaching a social gospel. It'll be so that these churches shall dry up; they will wither and fade away. Some will decline from thousands and in months will be gone and the property sold, because they're dead. They'll not exist in days to come.

"Oh, they have existed in the days past, because it's not been so, what will be so in the latter end. The anointing of God shall flow in the earth, and darkness shall prevail over those who are in darkness. The gross darkness shall cover those who are in darkness, but the light shall grow lighter to those who walk in the light.

"My Church shall be built, and it will be as though it were in a day. For I'll make a short work of righteousness in the earth."

Jesus Restores Man

John to the seven churches which are in Asia: Grace be unto you, and peace, from him which is, and which was, and which is to come; and from the seven Spirits which are before his throne; and from Jesus Christ, who is the faithful witness, and **the first begotten of the dead,** *and the prince of the kings of the earth* (Rev. 1:4,5).

Jesus is the Prince of the kings of the earth. Did you ever wonder *who* the kings are? I'll remind you. Paul said in Romans 5:17, *For if by one man's offence death reigned by one; much more they which receive abundance of grace and of the gift of righteousness shall* **reign in life** *by one, Jesus Christ.*

Jesus is the Prince and we are the kings—restored to our rightful place. Our authority is restored. *The Amplified Bible* says we shall ". . . reign as kings in life through the One, Jesus Christ."

God said in Genesis 22:16,17, *By myself have I sworn, saith the Lord, for* *because thou hast done this thing, and hast not withheld thy son, thine only son: That in blessing I will bless thee, and in multiplying I will multiply thy seed as the stars of the heaven, and as the sand which is upon the sea shore; and **thy seed shall possess the gate of his enemies.***

The Seed was Jesus. Galatians 3:13-16 says:

Christ hath redeemed us from the curse of the law, being made a curse for us: for it is written, Cursed is every one that hangeth on a tree:

That the blessing of Abraham might come on the Gentiles through Jesus Christ; that we might receive the promise of the Spirit through faith.

Brethren, I speak after the manner of men; Though it be but a man's covenant, yet if it be confirmed, no man disannulleth, or addeth thereto.

*Now to Abraham and his seed were the promises made. He saith not, And to seeds, as of many; but as of one, and to **thy seed, which is Christ.***

Paul is referring to *Christ, Who is the Seed,* Who shall possess the gate of His enemies. Verse 14 says, . . . *receive the promise of the Spirit through faith.*

Contrary to what most people believe, **he isn't talking about the Holy Spirit baptism. He is talking about the promise the Holy Spirit made to Abraham concerning his Seed, Jesus Christ.**

For ye are all the children of God by faith in Christ Jesus. For as many of you as have been baptized into Christ have put on Christ. There is neither Jew nor Greek, there is neither bond nor free, there is neither male nor female: for ye are all one in Christ Jesus. And if ye be Christ's, then are ye Abraham's seed (*seed,* not *seeds:* He is calling us, the Body of Christ, the seed of Abraham; we are one with Him) *and heirs according to the promise* (vv. 26-29).

We are heirs according to the promise, restored to our rightful godliness, with authority in this earth. We are born of the Spirit of God, quickened according to the Word of God—men under authority on earth—and we will possess the gate of our enemies.

Paul said in Ephesians 1:16-20:

I cease not to give thanks for you, making mention of you in my prayers; that the god of our Lord Jesus Christ, the Father of glory, may give unto you the spirit of wisdom and revelation in the knowledge of him: the eyes of your understanding being enlightened; that ye may know what is the hope of his calling, and what the riches of the glory of his inheritance in the saints, and what is the exceeding greatness of his power to us-ward who believe, according to the working of his mighty power, which he wrought in Christ, when he raised him from the dead.

Paul said, ''I don't want you ignorant *of the mighty power* that was wrought in Christ when He raised Him from the dead, because it's *the same power* that's going to raise people from spiritual *death* to spiritual *life* today, just like it did in that day.''

Even when we were dead in sins, hath quickened us together with Christ, (by grace ye are saved;) and hath raised us up together, and made us sit together in heavenly places in Christ Jesus (Eph. 2:5,6).

The reason He wants you to get hold of that mighty power which He wrought in Christ when He raised Him from the dead is because **when He raised you from spiritual death to**

spiritual life, He exalted you. As far as God is concerned, **He sees you seated on the right hand of the Father, with Jesus, in authority and power forever**—above all principalities and powers and might and dominion. Now, you realize we're not there in body, but we are there in **spiritual authority and power.**

Wherefore God also hath highly exalted him, and given him a name which is above every name: that at the name of Jesus every knee should bow, of things in heaven, and things in earth, and things under the earth (Phil. 2:9,10).

Jesus defeated Satan in mortal combat. He received that name by inheritance. It was bestowed upon Him. And **that name is above every name.** I want to remind you that **Jesus gave us His name to use!**

He stood on the mountain before He ascended to the Father and said, "All power is given unto Me both in heaven and in earth." (Matt. 28:18.) Then He turned to the believer and said, "Now, **you** go in My name. **You** cast out demons. **You** heal the sick. **You** raise the dead."(Mark 16:15-18.) In other words, "While I am gone, **you do it. You** strip Satan of his false authority."

Jesus had all the power in heaven and earth, and He gave it to the believer! He gave you His name, and the name of Jesus is above every name. The name of Jesus is above cancer, arthritis, and emphysema. It's above anything you can name. Every disease known to mankind has some sort of name, and the name of Jesus is above them *all!*

Sometimes people read the Scriptures and say, "Glory to God! Every knee will bow to Jesus!" but that's not what it says. Every knee shall bow to the **name** of Jesus, and He gave *you* that name to use.

David said in Psalm 138:2, . . . *thou hast magnified thy word above all thy name.* The name of Jesus is above every name, and every knee shall bow to that Name. The name of Jesus gives you authority in three worlds: over beings in heaven, beings in earth, and beings under the earth. **He has given believers authority in three worlds!** And not only that, but **God has magnified His Word above His name!**

God has given you authority in the earth. He has restored your authority through the rebirth of the human spirit. He has given to you that which Satan stole from Adam. God expects the believer to *occupy the earth* until He comes.

No, He didn't say, "Store up potatoes and hide in the mountains." He said, *Occupy till I come!* (Luke 19:13).

The United States occupied Germany after World War II. Do you think we went over and asked, "Well, what do you all want to do?" No! We occupied and controlled the place!

Jesus said for us *to occupy* and *control this earth* until He comes. We have the authority to do it. It will be done through His name and His Word.

Prophetic Word

Again, I share a prophetic utterance that came forth as I taught on this subject in one of my meetings. The Spirit of the Lord said:

"Stand to your feet in this day and hour. For this is the day for My wisdom and My power to be manifested in the earth. In the days to come, you'll see mighty manifestations, for the wealth of the sinner is laid up for the just.

"So begin to establish yourself upon My Word, for I've magnified My Word above My name. And as My name is above every name in the earth, so is My Word above every prophet of doom who would prophesy your destruction or the defeat of the Church.

"So rise to your feet and stretch yourself to your true height. For these are the days that My people shall walk in victory and shall enforce the defeat of the powers of darkness by My Word flowing from their lips.

"Men filled with the Spirit of God shall walk in the ways of My wisdom. Nations of the world will call to this nation and say, 'Send us a prophet of God so that we may see the things that we hear are happening there.' For the things that have worked in days past don't work in this time.

"As the prophet of God goes to minister, he will have the freedom to go behind the iron curtain. He will go behind the bamboo curtain. The knowledge of the Lord shall spread throughout the earth. You will see a great work in your day, for the wealth of the sinner will eventually find its way into your hands as you walk in the precepts of My Word. Establish yourself and stand to your true height in My Word, and watch Me perform in your day."

14
Keys of the Kingdom

In Matthew 16:16 Peter made this great confession: *Thou art the Christ, the Son of the living God.*

Jesus answered, *Flesh and blood hath not revealed it unto thee, but my Father which is in heaven. And I say also unto thee, That thou art Peter, and upon this rock I will build my church; and* **the gates of hell shall not prevail against it** (vv. 17,18).

Notice who Jesus said would build the Church. For years, man has tried to build it and has failed. Religious leaders thought *they* had built it with their synagogues and places of learning. But Jesus said, *I will build my church; and the gates of hell shall not prevail against it.*

Then He said, *I will give unto thee* **the keys of the kingdom** *of heaven: and whatsoever thou shalt bind on earth shall be bound in heaven: and whatsoever thou shalt* *loose on earth shall be loosed in heaven* (v. 19).

What does Jesus mean by "the keys *of* the Kingdom"? He didn't say, "keys *to* the Kingdom." If you had the key *to* a hotel, you could get in the lobby, but not into a single room. If you have the keys *of* the hotel, you could unlock every room in the building.

Verily I say unto you, There be some standing here, which shall not taste of death, till they see the Son of man coming in his kingdom (v. 28).

When I first read this verse, I wondered how Jesus could say the Church was going to be raptured before some of those people died.

Do you see how you can draw "religious thinking" out of that? But that wasn't what Jesus was saying. He said, "Some of you standing here shall not taste death until you see the Son of Man coming in His Kingdom." Jesus came forth from the grave, the firstborn among many brethren, and He came into His Kingdom.

Jesus said, . . . *The kingdom of God cometh not with observation . . . the kingdom of God is within you* (Luke

17:20,21). He was saying something very different from what most of us have thought. Even His closest disciples asked, "When will You restore the kingdom of Israel?"

Jesus said, "My Kingdom doesn't come with observation. It is within men." The born-again man is capable of operating on the same level of faith with God. He is a joint-heir with Jesus.

And if ye be Christ's then are ye Abraham's seed, and heirs according to the promise (Gal. 3:29). *What promise?* The promise that the Holy Spirit made to Abraham: **that his seed would possess the gate of his enemies.**

The Amplified Bible states Jesus' words in Matthew 16:19 this way: "I will give you the keys of the kingdom of heaven, and whatever you bind—that is, declare to be improper and unlawful—on earth must be already bound in heaven; and whatever you loose on earth—declare lawful—must be what is already loosed in heaven."

Someone might ask, "What good would that do if it is already bound up there?"

Jesus is saying, "I will give believers authority and power to loose things on earth that are allowed in heaven and to bind things on earth that are not allowed in heaven."

Just ask yourself, "What things are *not* allowed in heaven?" There is no sickness or disease in heaven, nor is there poverty. There is no evil, no lack of any kind. Heaven is a healthy, happy place.

Jesus said, "You have authority to bind evil forces upon earth that cause sickness, disease, poverty, and sin."

What is loosed in heaven? Life, health, abundance, happiness, joy, and peace. Now you can understand *why* Jesus called the power of binding and loosing *the keys of the Kingdom!*

The Kingdom Is Come

When Jesus was teaching His disciples some principles of prayer, He said, *After this manner therefore pray ye: Our Father which art in heaven, Hallowed be thy name. Thy kingdom come . . .* (Matt. 6:9,10).

This is a prayer under the Old Covenant. Jesus said, "Pray that the

Kingdom will come." Well, it has already come. The Kingdom is with born-again men. It's not going to come when we get to heaven; it's already here.

Again, Luke 17:20,21 says, *The kingdom of God cometh not with observation: Neither shall they say, Lo here! or, lo there! for, behold, the kingdom of God is within you.* We should reign as kings in life by Jesus Christ.

Jesus told His disciples to pray, *Thy kingdom come. Thy will be done in earth, as it is in heaven. Whose* will be done? God's will be done.

It's God's will that is to be done in earth as it is in heaven. We need to ask ourselves: How is it in heaven? There's no sickness in heaven—no disease, poverty, pain, or sorrow—so that is God's will for this earth. It must be His will for He told the disciples to pray that way.

You, as a believer, have the God-given right and ability to bind things that are bound in heaven. You have *authority* to come against these things. You have **delegated authority** to loose on earth *all things* that are loosed in heaven. Whatsoever you can bind on earth is what is bound *in heaven*. It is something **you** do.

Let me remind you of what Paul said in Galatians 3:29. *If ye be Christ's, then are ye Abraham's seed, and heirs according to the promise* (which the Holy Spirit made to Abraham).

God presents the blessings of obedience to the children of Israel in Deuteronomy 28:1-7.

And it shall come to pass, if thou shalt hearken diligently unto the voice of the Lord thy God, to observe and to do all his commandments which I command thee this day, that the Lord thy God will set thee on high above all nations of the earth: And all these blessings shall come on thee, and overtake thee, if thou shalt hearken unto the voice of the Lord thy God (vv. 1,2).

In other words, you can't run fast enough to get away from all the blessings if you'll hearken diligently to the voice of the Lord thy God. They will come behind you and overtake you.

Blessed shalt thou be in the city, and blessed shalt thou be in the field. Blessed shall be the fruit of thy body, and the fruit of thy ground, and the fruit of thy cattle, the increase of thy kine, and flocks of thy sheep.

Blessed shall be thy basket and thy store. Blessed shalt thou be when thou comest in, and blessed shalt thou be when thou goest out. The Lord shall cause thine enemies that rise up against thee to be smitten before thy face: they shall come out against thee one way, and shall flee before thee seven ways (vv. 3-7).

People read this and say, "Yes, but that was to Israel." Yes, it was. It was to the children of Israel. *But if ye be Christ's, then are ye Abraham's seed, and heirs according to the promise.* You have been restored to your rightful godliness.

Blessings Are For Our Use, Now

And the Lord thy God will make thee plenteous in every work of thine hand, in the fruit of thy body, and in the fruit of thy cattle, and in the fruit of thy land, for good: for the Lord will again rejoice over thee for good, as he rejoiced over thy fathers:

If thou shalt hearken unto the voice of the Lord thy God, to keep his commandments and his statutes which are written in this book of the law, and if thou turn unto the Lord thy God with all thine heart, and with all thy soul.

For this commandment which I command thee this day, it is not hidden from thee, neither is it far off.

Deuteronomy 30:9-11

Remember, Jesus said, "I will give you the keys *of* the Kingdom." Most people are putting off all the blessings until they get to heaven. They say, "When we get to heaven, we'll have all this power and authority."

What would you do with it *then*? There will be no demons there, no battles, no evil, no sickness. You won't need it then. You need it *now!* Those blessings He was talking about are not yours when you get to *heaven*; **they belong to you** *now.*

It is not in heaven, that thou shouldest say, Who shall go up for us to heaven, and bring it unto us, that we may hear it, and do it? Neither is it beyond the sea, that thou shouldest say, Who shall go over the sea for us, and bring it unto us, that we may hear it, and do it? But the word is very nigh unto thee, in thy mouth, and in thy heart, that thou mayest do it (vv. 12-14).

Notice, the Word gets in your *mouth first*, *then* it gets into your *heart*. The Apostle Paul said:

The word is nigh thee, even in thy mouth, and in thy heart: that is, the word of faith, which we preach; that if thou shalt confess with thy mouth the Lord Jesus, and shalt believe in thine heart that God hath raised him from the dead, thou shalt be saved (Rom. 10:8,9).

Blessings of God Are Not for All

This blessing God has promised is for those who have God's Word in their mouth. People who are born on earth have the right to choose their words. Angels are created beings and don't have that right.

Jesus said, "I give you the keys of the Kingdom, and whatsoever you bind on earth shall be bound in heaven." Man, restored to his rightful godlikeness, has the authority to dominate the earth.

Let me reiterate:

1. **Genesis 22:17:** . . . *thy seed shall possess the gate of his enemies.*

2. **Matthew 16:18:** *I will build my church and the gates of hell shall not prevail against it.*
3. **Colossians 1:17,18:** *And he is before all things, and by him all things consist. And he is the head of the body, the church:* **who is the beginning,** *the firstborn from the dead. . . .*

Jesus was the beginning of the Church. He is the Head of the Church. He started His Church in the gates of hell to prove that the gates of hell wouldn't prevail against it.

He entered into the gates of hell (Hades)—the place, but not the *final* abode, of the wicked dead. They are going to be cast into the lake of fire, which burns forever. The place Jesus went into was not literally the lake of fire; it was the gate to the place.

Jesus was born again in the pit of hell. He was the firstborn, the first-begotten, from the dead. **He started the Church of the firstborn in the gates of hell.**

I marvel at God's wisdom when I step back and look at the whole picture. He didn't wait until later to destroy the power of hell. He went down to the gates and started His Church there. Jesus is *the Head* of the Church. He is its *beginning*. The Church started when Jesus was born again in the gates of hell. He is the firstborn among many brethren.

If Satan could stop people from being born again, he would have stopped Jesus first when Jesus was in hell. But Satan was no match for the Word of God.

The Devil isn't too smart. He doesn't even have the keys to his own house; Jesus has them! Jesus stripped Satan of the keys of death, hell, and the grave; then He tore the gates off that place when He left!

Paul said, *If thou shalt confess with thy mouth the Lord Jesus, and shalt believe in thine heart that God hath raised him from the dead, thou shalt be saved* (Rom. 10:9). There are not enough demons in hell to stop people from being born again if they will confess from their hearts Jesus as Lord of their lives.

Be Strong in the Lord

Finally, my brethren, be strong in the Lord, and in the power of his might (Eph. 6:10). Paul didn't say anything about being strong in yourself.

Someone may say, "I'm trying to be strong." Well, he said for us to *be strong in the Lord, and in the power of his might*—not *try* to be.

Put on the whole armour of God, that ye may be able to stand against the wiles of the devil (v. 11). The word *whole* means "complete." Put on the **complete** armor of God that you *may be able to stand* against the wiles of the Devil.

What is Paul talking about? Isaiah 59:17 refers to being clothed with righteousness. Paul begins to name God's clothes (God's armor). This armor is spiritual clothing.

For we wrestle not against flesh and blood, but against principalities, against powers, against the rulers of the darkness of this world, against spiritual wickedness in high places.

Wherefore take unto you the whole armour of God, that ye may be able to withstand in the evil day, and having done all, to stand.

Stand therefore, having your loins girt about with truth, and having on the breastplate of righteousness;

And your feet shod with the preparation of the gospel of peace;

Above all, taking the shield of faith, wherewith ye shall be able to quench all the fiery darts of the wicked.

And take the helmet of salvation, and the sword of the Spirit, which is the word of God.

Ephesians 6:12-17

God's Word is the sword of the *human* spirit, not the sword of the *Holy* Spirit. Get God's Word into your spirit and speak it. Then it becomes a sword in your mouth. The Bible itself is not the sword of the Spirit; but when you get this Word in your spirit and speak it out your mouth, it becomes the sword of the *human* spirit.

The Apostle John wrote in 1 John 4:4, *Ye are of God, little children, and have overcome them: because greater is he that is in you, than he that is in the world.* It says, *. . . and have overcome them.* You're not *going to* do it sometime. You *are* restored to your rightful place. You have God's clothes on.

Wouldn't it be something if we put on the helmet of salvation and the breastplate of righteousness, girt our loins about with truth, shod our feet with the preparation of the Gospel of peace, took the sword of the Spirit (the Word of God), and ran away to hide in the mountains?

No, we're not going to hide in the mountains! We're going to "occupy till He comes." Then we're going to be with Jesus, for we are the family of God. He is coming after a Church without spot, or wrinkle, or any such thing. He is seated at the right hand of the Father until His enemies are made His footstool.

15
Dominion
In Three Worlds

To have dominion in the earth requires a physical body. We have previously discussed the words of Jesus in John, chapter 10; but, because of that scripture's importance, I wish to emphasize it again. Jesus said, . . . *He that entereth not by the door into the sheepfold, but climbeth up some other way, the same is a thief and a robber. But he that entereth in by the door is the shepherd of the sheep* (John 10:1,2).

Satan is the one who entered in some other way. **He was not born in the earth.** The only legal way to get into this earth with authority is to be born here. Even angels can't preach the Gospel in the earth. They don't have that authority.

We can't send the Holy Ghost to Africa to preach the Gospel; the Holy Ghost doesn't have a body. **You** *are the* *one with the body, and* **you** *have the authority!* When *your authority* and *God's ability* get together, **all things are possible.**

Satan is the thief and robber. Jesus is the Good Shepherd. Jesus was born here; He entered in by the door of human birth. Jesus had the authority of a man.

Legal Entry into Earth

The door in verse 1 is not the same door in verse 7. This is a progressive story. Jesus came by the legal entry, through birth. He had all the authority of a man. He lived as a man and was anointed with the Holy Ghost. He went before us and destroyed the Devil's works. He went to the cross, gave up His life, and became the supreme sacrifice, which leads to the progressive part in verse 7: *Verily, verily, I say unto you, I am the door of the sheep.*

Because He suffered and died spiritually for us, He was born again and called *the firstborn from the dead* (Col. 1:18); *the firstborn among many brethren* (Rom. 8:29); and *the first begotten from the dead* (Rev. 1:5). Jesus was born again, and He has become the door.

The fleshly birth is the legal entry into the earth. But because Jesus is the Head of the Church and the firstborn from the dead, He became the door, or legal entry, into the Kingdom of God. There is no other way. You can't get there by a church door. You can't get there by being baptized. You can't get there by paying your tithes or by being good. **You must be born again, and Jesus is the door of that new birth!**

Just as *physical* birth is the legal entry into earth, the *spiritual* birth through Jesus Christ is the *only* legal way into heaven.

After Jesus rose from the dead, He went back by the tomb to get His body. He was now the Risen Christ, the firstborn from the dead, the firstborn among many brethren. He talked to Mary Magdalene early the third day.

She, supposing him to be the gardener, saith unto him, Sir, if thou have borne him hence, tell me where thou hast laid him, and I will take him away. Jesus saith unto her, Mary. She turned herself, and saith unto him, Rabboni; which is to say, Master. Jesus

*saith unto her, Touch me not; for I am not
yet ascended to my Father: but go to my
brethren . . .* (John 20:15-17).

To understand this, we must go to
Hebrews, chapter 9:

*But Christ being come an high priest of
good things to come, by a greater and more
perfect tabernacle, not made with hands,
that is to say, not of this building; neither by
the blood of goats and calves, but **by his
own blood he entered in once into the
holy place, having obtained eternal
redemption for us*** (vv. 11,12).

*For if the blood of bulls and of goats, and
the ashes of an heifer sprinkling the unclean,
sanctifieth to the purifying of the flesh: **how
much more** shall the blood of Christ, who
through the eternal Spirit offered himself
without spot to God, **purge your
conscience from dead works** to serve the
living God?* (vv. 13,14).

*For Christ is not entered into the holy
places made with hands, which are the
figures of the true; but into heaven itself,
now to appear in the presence of God for us*
(v. 24).

We are being well represented at the
throne of God. He didn't do anything
for Himself; *He did all of it for us.* Jesus is

appearing right now, in the presence of God, for *us.*

Let's read now from Hebrews, chapter 9: *Nor yet that he should offer himself often, as the high priest entereth into the holy place every year with blood of others; for then must he often have suffered since the foundation of the world: but now once in the end of the world hath he appeared to put away sin by the sacrifice of himself* (vv. 25,26).

Jesus put away sin by the sacrifice of Himself. Sin has no domination over you. *And as it is appointed unto men once to die, but after this the judgment: so Christ was once offered to bear the sins of many; and unto them that look for him shall he appear the second time without sin unto salvation* (vv. 27,28).

What does it mean that He would appear without sin? Jesus never sinned. But He did *become* sin after He died physically on the cross. He will appear the second time *without sin.*

In chapter 20 of John, Jesus said, *I am not yet ascended . . .* (v. 17). After that, He did ascend to the Father. He carried **His own blood** into the Holy of Holies and sprinkled that blood on the mercy seat. **God accepted that blood as the final atonement, and Jesus obtained** *eternal redemption* **for us.**

Peace Be Unto You

Somewhere between the time Jesus appeared to Mary and the time He appeared to Thomas, Jesus ascended to the heavens.

Isaiah 53:5 in *The Amplified Bible* says, ''. . . The chastisement needful to obtain peace and well-being for us, was upon him.''

The first thing Jesus said when He came to His disciples was, *Peace be unto you* (John 20:19). He showed them His hands and His side. *Then said Jesus to them again, Peace be unto you: as my Father hath sent me, even so send I you* (v. 21).

Jesus was delegating authority to His body of believers.

And when he had said this, he breathed on them, and saith unto them, Receive ye the Holy Ghost . . .

But Thomas, one of the twelve, called Didymus, was not with them when Jesus came. The other disciples therefore said unto him, We have seen the Lord. But he said unto them, Except I shall see in his hands

*the print of the nails, and put my finger into
the print of the nails, and thrust my hand
into his side, I will not believe.*

*And after eight days again his disciples
were within, and Thomas with them: then
came Jesus, the doors being shut, and stood
in the midst, and said, Peace be unto you.*

*Then saith he to Thomas, Reach hither
thy finger, and behold my hands; and reach
hither thy hand, and thrust it into my
side: and be not faithless, but believing.*

*And Thomas answered and said unto
him, My Lord and my God* (vv. 22-28).

When Jesus came to earth, He gave
up His divine power. He came as a man
and took upon Himself the body of a
man. **He was deity here, but He did not
operate in divine power. He operated
in the authority of a man anointed with
the Holy Ghost.**

After Jesus was resurrected, He had
a glorified body. He sat down and ate
with the disciples, then got up and
walked through the wall.

But here is something we haven't
seen. We have the idea that when Jesus
rose from the dead, He was perfectly
whole. But the holes were still in His
side. He could hold His hands up, and

you could see daylight through them. Those holes are *still* in His hands. He has the body of a man and will have the body of a man through all eternity.

Jesus became as we *were* that we might be as He is *now.* He took on Himself the body of a man, and the Bible says you'll see *the Son of man coming in the clouds* (Mark 13:26).

He became a man that we might be joint-heirs with Him. Scars are still on His back from the terrible lashing He received. He said to His disciples, *Handle me, and see; for a spirit hath not flesh and bones, as ye see me have* (Luke 24:39).

He told Mary, "Don't touch Me; I have not yet ascended." But now He *has* ascended. He *has* obtained eternal redemption for us! He came back and breathed on His disciples and said, *Receive ye the Holy Ghost.* Why?

Jesus said, . . . *the works that I do, shall he do also; and greater works than these shall he do; because I go unto my Father* (John 14:12).

What does Jesus' going to the Father have to do with it? He said, *If I go not away, the Comforter will not come unto you;*

but if I depart, I will send him unto you (John 16:7).

Paul said in 1 Corinthians 12:27, *Now ye are the body of Christ, and members in particular.* Jesus has ascended to the Father. The only physical body He has on earth is yours. **Your body is the authority God has in the earth today.** *You* are the one with the body! *You* are the one with *authority* in the earth, and *He* is the One with the *power!*

Jesus said, "I'm going to send the Holy Ghost (the ability of God) to reside in you. Then you will have the authority and the ability to destroy the works of the Devil." In other words, "If you'll let Me use your body, I'll let you use My ability." That's bad news for Satan any way you look at it!

Jesus said, "If you love me, you'll keep my commandments, and we will come and make our abode with you." (John 14:21,23.) The Father, Son, and Holy Ghost will set up camp inside you.

Any person who is born of the Spirit of God and recreated in the image of God is capable of operating on the same level of faith with God. He has the power source of the Father, Son, and Holy Ghost residing in his spirit.

That still was not enough to satisfy Him. Jesus said, *I have yet many things to say unto you, but you cannot bear them now. Howbeit when he, the Spirit of truth, is come, he will guide you into all truth . . . and he will shew you things to come . . . All things that the Father hath are mine: therefore said I, that he shall take of mine, and shall shew it unto you* (John 16:12-15).

Jesus was the glorified Christ. He could walk through doors; He could appear wherever He wished; and there was something else different about Jesus: The disciples could see the holes in His hands and in His side. But Jesus had said, ''A spirit hath not flesh and bone as I have.''

Jesus' body is composed of flesh and bone—not flesh and blood. He has a glorified body that does not operate on the blood system. It is flesh and bone. Christ, in His glorified body and divine power, *lost His right to minister in the earth.*

There is something strange about it all. After Jesus rose from the dead, and until He ascended to the Father, *He did not do a single miracle!* He healed no one, cast out no demons, and raised no one from the dead. Why? Because He had become the *glorified Christ*. He had His glorified body and His divine power. *He had lost His right to minister anymore on earth as a man.* He was restored to His Godhead powers. He no longer had the body of a natural man; He had a glorified body.

Satan Has No Authority— He Has No Body Here

It's time for the Church to get a revelation of this: **Satan doesn't have a body and therefore has no authority on earth!**

Jesus is speaking in John 12:31 (before He went to the cross) and says, *Now is the judgment of this world: now shall the prince of this world be cast out.* The word for *judgment* is the Greek word *krisis* and is translated into the English language as "crisis." *Crisis* means "a turning point." Jesus was saying, "Now is *the turning point* of this world. Now shall the prince of this world system be cast out."

And there was war in heaven: Michael and his angels fought against the dragon; and the dragon fought and his angels, and prevailed not; neither was their place found any more in heaven.

And the great dragon was cast out, that old serpent, called the Devil, and Satan, which deceiveth the whole world: he was cast out into the earth, and his angels were cast out with him.

And I heard a loud voice saying in heaven, Now is come salvation, and strength, and the kingdom of our God, and the power of his Christ: for the accuser of our brethren is cast down, which accused them before our God day and night.

Revelation 12:7-10

I always thought this was a future event, but evidently it took place when Jesus ascended to the throne. There's no doubt Who ascended to the throne or who the dragon was that was cast out. What Jesus didn't do in hell, He finished in heaven!

And they overcame him by the blood of the Lamb, and by the word of their testimony; and they loved not their lives unto the death. Therefore rejoice, ye heavens, and ye that dwell in them. Woe to

the inhabiters of the earth and of the sea! for
the devil is come down unto you, having
great wrath, because he knoweth that he
hath but a short time (vv. 11,12).

At this point, Satan was cast out of
heaven. He no longer accuses us before
the Father. There was no place in
heaven for him. The reason Satan
wasn't cast down to the earth before
was because men of earth didn't have
the ability to handle him. They weren't
born again. They were operating under
the Old Covenant.

The only people really able to handle
Satan in the four Gospels were the men
Jesus had anointed. Remember that He
called seventy of them together and
anointed them, then sent them out to
heal the sick, raise the dead, and cast
out demons. (See Luke 10:1-9.)

Those men were legally born in
earth, and their bodies gave them
authority. God gave them the ability.
The anointing of God worked through
them to bring healing to the sick, to cast
out demons, and to raise the dead.

A Footstool Under His Feet

But this man, after he had offered one sacrifice for sins for ever, sat down on the right hand of God; from henceforth expecting till his enemies be made his footstool (Heb. 10:12,13).

The Greek states, ". . . waiting until He places His enemies as a footstool under His feet." Don't get too excited about going to heaven right now. There are a few things that must take place first. **The enemy must be put under our feet!**

The Scriptures plainly state, "He is seated at the right hand of the Father until His enemies be made His footstool." Jesus will leave there one day, and we are going to meet Him in the air. But He is seated there now *until* His enemies are put under His feet.

Jesus is the Head, and you (the Church) are the Body. A footstool is used to put your feet on. *We're going to put our feet on Satan!* It's going to be that way before Jesus removes Himself from the right hand of the Father.

In chapter 28 of Matthew, we see Jesus as He stood on the mountain. He was about to ascend to the Father. Let's pay close attention to what He said.

And when they saw him, they worshipped him: but some doubted. And Jesus came and spake unto them, saying, All power is given unto me in heaven and in earth (vv. 17,18).

Notice, Jesus said *all* power. If He *has all power*, then there just *ain't no more!* That isn't good English, but it puts the point over. **Jesus had all the power!**

Then He said, *Go ye therefore, and teach all nations, baptizing them in the name of the Father, and of the Son, and of the Holy Ghost: teaching them to observe all things whatsoever I have commanded you: and, lo, I am with you alway, even unto the end of the world* (vv. 19,20).

Chapter 16 of Mark records the same incident:

And he said unto them, Go ye into all the world, and preach the gospel to every creature. He that believeth and is baptized shall be saved; but he that believeth not shall be damned. And these signs shall follow them that believe; in my name shall they cast out devils; they shall speak with new tongues; they shall take up serpents; and if they drink any deadly thing, it shall not hurt them; they shall lay hands on the sick, and they shall recover (Mark 16:15-18).

Jesus is not talking about handling a snake. He is saying, "If that old serpent, Satan, invades your home, *you cast him out!*" He isn't talking about going on demon hunts or devil chases. He means *you* are the one to cast out Satan. *You* have the authority to do so. Satan is an outlaw here. He has no authority in the earth. **The only place he can dominate and control is where people allow him to do so.** (Lack of knowledge is the main reason.)

If you want to know what Jesus taught in the Great Commission, read chapters 9 and 10 of Matthew's Gospel and see what He commanded. The Church, as a whole, has never seen it and has never set out to do it.

And Jesus went about all the cities and villages, teaching in their synagogues, and preaching the gospel of the kingdom, and healing every sickness and every disease among the people.

But when he saw the multitudes, he was moved with compassion on them, because they fainted, and were scattered abroad, as sheep having no shepherd.

Then saith he unto his disciples, The harvest truly is plenteous, but the labourers are few; pray ye therefore the Lord of the harvest, that he will send forth labourers into his harvest (Matt. 9:35-38).

When most people read this scriptural passage, they think about going out preaching to get people saved. That's not what Jesus is talking about here. He is saying, ''There are many sick, many lame, many possessed with demons.'' You will notice that Jesus was doing these things: healing the sick, raising the dead, and casting out demons. Now, of course, the saving of the lost is involved here, but that is the *result* of obeying the first part.

And when he had called unto him his twelve disciples, he gave them power against unclean spirits, to cast them out, and to heal all manner of sickness and all manner of disease (Matt. 10:1).

He sent some laborers into the harvest field. *And as ye go, preach, saying, The kingdom of heaven is at hand. Heal the sick, cleanse the lepers, raise the dead, cast out devils: freely ye have received, freely give* (vv. 7,8).

We Need to Obey
The Great Commission

The Great Commission is "to teach all nations to obey whatsoever I have commanded you."

When the Church begins to obey the Great Commission, we will teach all nations to heal the sick, raise the dead, and cast out demons. *The revival will be on!* Raise a few dead and you won't have to advertise your meetings. Sinners will come from far and near to be born again.

You won't have to preach three hours to get it done. Just get a few people healed, a few cripples walking, a few of the dead raised, and multitudes will come. Then, while you are trying to eat a quiet meal at home, there will be thousands outside trying to get in to hear what you have to say.

Jesus never had to advertise a meeting. He tried, at times, to go into the mountains for rest, and five thousand people showed up out there to hear Him. *His Word was with power.*

When we begin to do what Jesus said for us to do, it will be the same in this day.

Notice, the whole tenth chapter of Matthew is the commandment Jesus was talking about: "Go . . . teach all nations . . . ."

And it came to pass, when Jesus had made an end of commanding his twelve disciples, he departed thence to teach and to preach in their cities (Matt. 11:1).

Then began he to upbraid the cities wherein most of his mighty works were done, because they repented not: Woe unto thee, Chorazin! woe unto thee, Bethsaida! for if the mighty works, which were done in you, had been done in Tyre and Sidon, they would have repented long ago in sackcloth and ashes. But I say unto you, It shall be more tolerable for Tyre and Sidon at the day of judgment, than for you (vv. 20-22).

Listen to the words of Jesus, "If I had healed the sick and raised the dead in Tyre and Sidon, as I did in other places, those people would have repented long ago." In other words, Jesus is saying that the reason people in Tyre and Sidon were not saved was because there weren't enough laborers to heal their sick and raise their dead. If the mighty works of God had been done in those cities, they would have repented and turned to God.

One reason more people are *not* turning to God today is because they see the religious mess this world is in. They see the false front. They see the *club houses* we call "churches" that have a form of godliness but deny the power, deny the virgin birth, deny the blood of Jesus. They don't see their needs being met.

When you begin to meet the needs of the people through the Word, prayer, and ministry, they will come by the thousands to be saved.

Jesus met every need of humanity while He was here on earth. Should we do any less? He has given us His name.

The Name of Jesus

God, who at sundry times and in divers manners spake in time past unto the fathers by the prophets, hath in these last days spoken unto us by his Son, whom he hath appointed heir of all things, by whom also he made the worlds;

Who being the brightness of his glory, and the express image of his person, and upholding all things by the word of his power, when he had by himself purged our sins, sat down on the right hand of the Majesty on high; being made so much better than the angels, as he hath by inheritance obtained a more excellent name than they (Heb. 1:1-4).

Jesus obtained His name in three ways: He inherited it; He earned it by conquest; and it was bestowed upon Him.

He inherited it from God, the Father. *Let this mind be in you, which was also in Christ Jesus: who being in the form of God, thought it not robbery to be equal with God* (Phil. 2:5,6). Even though Jesus was a man, He didn't consider it robbery to do the same works as God.

In the beginning was the Word, and the Word was with God, and the Word was God (John 1:1). Jesus said, "I and My Father are one."

But made himself of no reputation (the Greek says He emptied Himself of that divine power when He came to this earth), *and took upon him, the form of a servant, and was made in the likeness of* men: and being found in fashion as a man, he humbled himself, and became obedient unto death, even the death of the cross.

Wherefore God also hath highly exalted him, and given him a name which is above every name: that at the name of Jesus every knee should bow, of **things** in heaven, and **things** in earth, and **things** under the earth; and that every tongue should confess that Jesus Christ is Lord, to the glory of God the Father (Phil. 2:7-11).

The word *things* should really be translated ''beings.'' In the Bible, *things* is italicized which means that it was added by translators. *Things* do not have knees.

Let's read it like this: ''That at the name of Jesus every knee should bow, of *beings* in heaven, *beings* in earth, and *beings* under the earth; and that every tongue should confess that Jesus Christ is Lord, to the glory of God, the Father.''

Someone said, ''Yes, that will happen when we get to heaven. Then we're going to have the name of Jesus and all that authority.''

Well, that might sound good, but let's read verses 14-16: *Do all things without murmurings and disputings: that ye may be blameless and harmless, the sons of God, without rebuke, in the midst of a crooked and perverse nation, among whom ye shine as lights in the world; holding forth the word of life . . . .*

There won't be a crooked and perverse nation in heaven. He is saying **man has authority to operate with legal authority in three worlds from the earth.** We have read this scripture and said, "Glory to God, every knee will bow to Jesus someday, in the sweet by-and-by."

It doesn't say that! It says, "Every knee will bow to the *name* of Jesus." **And He gave us His name to use!** *These signs shall follow them that believe; in my name shall they cast out devils; they shall speak with new tongues . . . they shall lay hands on the sick, and they shall recover* (Mark 16:17,18).

You Have Authority

The name of Jesus has authority, not only in this earth, but in all three worlds. The Body of Christ stands in a unique position in this dispensation of having authority in all three worlds.

Delegated authority was given to us by Jesus Himself, so that we can fulfill the Great Commission. We have authority for three reasons:

1. **We have been born of flesh.** That has given us a body which makes us legal on earth.

2. **We have been born of the Spirit,** which gives us the anointing from God.

3. **Jesus has bestowed His name upon us.** We have authority to use the name of Jesus as if it were our very own!

And the glory which thou gavest me I have given them; that they may be one, even as we are one (John 17:22).

He said that every knee should bow: of beings *in heaven*, beings *in the earth*, and beings *under the earth* including principalities, powers, and rulers of darkness.

We stand in a unique position through that Name. We can summon the aid *of all heaven to work in our behalf*. He said in *that day* we would ask Him nothing, but whatsoever we would ask the Father, He would give it to us.

Now He abides on earth in the Person of the Holy Spirit. All heaven is at *your* disposal. Whatsoever *you* bind on earth shall be bound in heaven.

Believers on earth have authority to use the mighty name of Jesus to bind certain things *from earth*. We can bind the principalities, the powers, and the rulers of darkness. We can loose things on this earth that have already been loosed in heaven because *we have the authority and the Name that is above every name—Jesus.*

16
One With God

Today the born-again believer stands in the unique position of having dominion in three worlds by being one with Christ.

That they all may be one; as thou, Father, art in me, and I thee, that they also may be one in us: that the world may believe that thou hast sent me.

And the glory which thou gavest me I have given them; that they may be one, even as we are one: I in them, and thou in me, that they may be made perfect in one; and that the world may know that thou hast sent me, and hast loved them, as thou hast loved me.

John 17:21-23

You have the right to come boldly before the throne of grace that you may obtain. You have authority to bind forces of evil that come against you on earth. The powers of darkness, demons, and outlaw spirits have no authority in the earth unless you give them authority.

There's a parallel of Adam and the believer. As Adam stood in the beginning, so the Church stands today. Adam had authority to say, "In the name of Almighty God, Satan, depart this planet forever!" But he didn't. He failed to use his authority, so he lost it.

The Church stands today in a parallel position. **We can use our authority or turn it over to Satan and allow him to operate on it.** The difference is that when Adam lost his authority, every person born on earth lost it. It had to be restored. But, today, if I fail to use my authority, you don't lose yours. *Any born-again man who desires to use the name of Jesus and proclaim the authority God has invested in him* **can do so with results!**

But the person who refuses to act on his authority permits Satan to *run roughshod over him.* He has denied his authority, and Satan uses that as an opportunity to kill, steal, and destroy.

Satan Cheats Christians When They Permit It

Recently I heard a certain individual testify how she had prayed to God for a closer walk with Him. She was willing to give up anything in life for that closer walk, except her husband. After a period of time, she became more desperate. She finally prayed, "Lord, I'll even be willing to give up my husband to be closer to You." (Matthew 19:6 says, *What therefore God hath joined together, let no man put asunder.*) In a short time her husband was dead.

She turned her authority over to Satan. She had authority to bind evil forces that would steal; *but with the words of her mouth she prayed foolishly and loosed Satan's ability.* That was a totally unscriptural dedication; it was a lack of knowledge that allowed Satan to steal her mate. You are not required to think that way. There was no way she could use her faith, because she thought God did it. No bigger lie has ever been told.

Christians are allowing Satan to run roughshod over them! *My people are destroyed for lack of knowledge* (Hos. 4:6).

Learn that *your body gives you authority in this earth*, and *the name of Jesus gives you authority to move heaven in your behalf!*

Satan can do very little unless he can find a body to use. He would tear up the earth in a minute if he could. But spirits can't do that; they must get into a body. That is *why* the world is in such a mess. Satan has entered wicked men, and wicked men are destroying the earth. **Don't blame it on God!**

As a born-again believer, your body and the name of Jesus give you *authority in three worlds*. **A man with authority to use the name of Jesus is one of the most powerful individuals on earth today**—far more powerful than evil spirits, demons, principalities, powers, or rulers of darkness. Man is God's power tool if he will be obedient and let God work through him. God must have a body to work through.

Paul said, ''Know ye not that your body is the temple of the Holy Ghost?'' (1 Cor. 3:16.) It is *the dwelling place* of the Holy Ghost. We have prayed for God to send the Holy Ghost to get someone saved, but the Holy Ghost won't go unless *we* go.

God dwells in you. Jesus said, . . . *If a man love me, he will keep my words: and my Father will love him, and we will come unto him, and make our abode with him* (John 14:23).

God is in every believer, and *with God all things are possible* (Matt. 19:26). The Bible says the Holy Spirit is a "Helper," a "Comforter," and "the One called alongside to help."

I am reminded of a carpenter who hired a helper. The carpenter told the helper, "Bring that ladder over here, and let's put up some sheetrock."

"I'm not gonna do it," the helper replied.

"Why not?" asked the carpenter. "You're my helper."

"Yes," he said. "I'm your helper, and I'll *help* you do it. But I'm not going to do it by myself."

We have tried to make an errand boy out of the Holy Ghost. **He is the power source, but He won't go without a body.**

What did Paul mean when he said, *We wrestle not against flesh and blood, but against principalities, against powers, against the rulers of the darkness of this world?*

He is telling us that when we come against wicked men doing evil, we shouldn't get mad at those men, but recognize that the Devil is operating through them. If we try to fight the wicked men, there will be only trouble.

This is a spiritual battle. Men have authority to use the name of Jesus in order to break powers that influence them. *We have authority in the name of Jesus to break powers of darkness that rule men today.*

We find the born-again man in a unique position today. He is the agent God anoints and uses to bring forth manifestations of His power.

Jesus Is Head of the Body

We read of this in Ephesians 1:16-23:

(I) cease not to give thanks for you, making mention of you in my prayers; that the God of our Lord Jesus Christ, the Father of glory, may give unto you the spirit of wisdom and revelation in the knowledge of him:

The eyes of your understanding being enlightened; that ye may know what is the hope of his calling, and what the riches of the glory of his inheritance in the saints,

And what is the exceeding greatness of his power to us-ward who believe, according to the working of his mighty power, which he wrought in Christ, when he raised him from the dead, and set him at his own right hand in the heavenly places,

Far above all principality, and power, and might, and dominion, and every name that is named, not only in this world, but also in that which is to come:

And hath put all things under his feet, and gave him to be the head over all things to the church, which is his body, the fulness of him that filleth all in all.

Notice, Jesus is the Head of the Church. The Church is His Body. He has put all things under His feet. The feet are in the Body, and you are the Body of Christ. *Now ye are the body of Christ, and members in particular* (1 Cor. 12:27). **As the Body, you have authority.**

And you hath he quickened, who were dead in trespasses and sins . . . Even when we were dead in sins, hath quickened us together with Christ, (by grace ye are saved;) and hath raised us up together, and made us sit together in heavenly places in Christ Jesus (Eph. 2:1,5,6).

Paul is saying, "He has quickened us (made us alive) together with Him. We are made *one* with Him. He has raised us up together with Him. When Jesus was seated at the right hand of the Father—far above all principality, and power, and might, and dominion—that was when *you were raised up and seated there*, in power and in authority with Jesus. We are one with Him."

We're not seated there physically. Our bodies are not there yet. But Jesus is there to appear in the presence of God for us. He is *there*, representing us in heaven, as we represent Him *here* on earth.

We (the Body) are representing Jesus on earth. In so many words Jesus said, "If you will represent Me there on earth, I will represent you here in heaven." You are well represented there. As far as God is concerned, you are seated at the right hand of the Father in spiritual power with Christ Jesus.

That in the ages to come he might shew the exceeding riches of his grace in his kindness toward us through Christ Jesus (v. 7).

Somebody said, " 'In the ages to come' is when we get to heaven." No. When you get to heaven, there won't be any ages or time. Time shall be no more. He is talking about this dispensation of grace. He is showing us the exceeding riches of His grace *now*.

As we read verse 10, our hearts can hardly grasp such awesome truth. *For we are his workmanship, created in Christ Jesus unto good works* (not made, created), *which God hath before ordained that we should walk in them.*

You can understand why John said in 1 John 4:4, *Ye are of God, little children, and have overcome them. . . .*

Overcome *who*? The principalities, powers, rulers of darkness, the Antichrist, and all other demon powers. As far as God is concerned, you have been raised up and made to sit in heavenly places in Christ Jesus.

He has raised us up and we are seated there in authority. *Jesus is far above all powers, and so are you,* **if you are**

in Christ, through the mighty name of Jesus, because *greater is he that is in you, than he that is in the world* (v. 4). The Greater One is *in you!* The one in the world is not so great—he is *defeated.*

Herein is our love made perfect, that we may have boldness in the day of judgment: because as he is, so are we in this world (v. 17).

Paul said Jesus was seated at the right hand of the Father far above all principalities, power, might, and dominion. That is where Jesus is today. And as Jesus is, so are we *now* in this world. Even while we are living in this world, *we are far above all evil forces through the name of Jesus.* There is power in that Name!

This Man Called Peter

If you have doubts, study the book of Acts. Peter was a man who could do nothing right. The first part of his life he was a failure going somewhere to happen. He went fishing and fished on the wrong side of the boat. Jesus told him to throw his net on the other side. Then, he caught so many fish that his net broke!

He ran a race to Jesus' tomb and lost. Peter seemed to be an almost hopeless case. When he opened his mouth, he put his foot in it. "I'll never deny You!" he said. "I'll die for You!" Then, he denied Jesus three times. He even cursed about it.

But this man was in the upper room when the Holy Ghost came. He was filled with the Holy Ghost and spoke with tongues. The Holy Ghost charged the *spirit man* inside him, and he received the ability and power of God.

He and John went to the temple to pray, and to the first crippled man they met Peter said, "Man, I don't have any money, but I'll tell you one thing, what I do have, I'll give to you: **In the name of Jesus, rise up and walk!**" (Acts 3:6.)

What *did* Peter have? *He had the name of Jesus.* He had the body that gave him authority to use that Name. *In the name of Jesus Christ of Nazareth, rise up and walk.*

That old boy misunderstood Peter. He *jumped up* and started leaping and praising God. That's not bad for a starter. Peter could do nothing right until he found out he had authority to use the name of Jesus. Peter exercised his authority over the world of darkness. There's no doubt that Satan had bound this man for forty years, but *the name of Jesus penetrated that darkness and loosed him.*

The Name Used at Lydda

In the ninth chapter of Acts you can see where Peter went to visit the saints that dwelt at Lydda. There he found a crippled man kept to this bed eight years, sick of the palsy. (You would have been sick of the palsy, too, if you'd had it for eight years!)

Notice that these were the saints who dwelt at Lydda. The man sick with the palsy was a born-again, tongue-talking Christian, but he was sick. I can imagine Peter saying something like this: "Let me remind you of something, Aeneas. Jesus Christ is making you *whole.*"

I can imagine Aeneas saying, "You know, I believe you are right!" Then he just gathered up his bed and went home. All Peter did was remind him that Jesus Christ had made him whole.

The name of Jesus will *devastate* the world of darkness by *exposing* it to light.

Tabitha Raised

It wasn't long until a lady named Tabitha died. Instead of calling the undertaker, they called for Peter. He went there and prayed. I don't know *what* he prayed, but I believe I know *how* he prayed. I imagine he prayed in tongues. I know *I* would have in a similar situation! Then Peter turned around and said, *Tabitha, arise* (Acts 9:40).

Peter spoke into another world and said, "You come back." Tabitha's spirit obeyed him and came back. A man with authority in more than one world had exercised *his authority* and *God's ability*.

A man with authority can call into **the heavens** for heavenly intervention! He can call to **the region of the damned** and tell them to loose and let go! He can call into **the spirit world** and bring back the spirit into the body **because of what Jesus did for us!**

Jesus Gave His Name To Be Used

Jesus has never used that Name for His own benefit. It is always used for others.

Beloved, now are we the sons of God, and it doth not yet appear what we shall be: but we know that, when he shall appear, we shall be like him; for we shall see him as he is (1 John 3:2).

I think we have put on our religious eyeglasses every time we have read this and said, "Yes, when Jesus appears, we shall be changed and made like Him." That is religious thinking and *not* what the Word says. *When he shall appear, we shall* (already) *be like him* (1 John 3:2). *We* are going to have Satan under our feet. Jesus is seated at the right hand of the Father *until His enemies are made His footstool!*

The Body of Christ must recognize they *have* authority in all three worlds. Jesus is going to stay seated at the right hand of the Father until we get busy and exercise our authority and His ability to destroy the work of the Devil. We must act on the words of Jesus, "Heal the sick, raise the dead, and cast out demons," *until He comes!*

Remember, Jesus said to His disciples, *Occupy till I come.* That doesn't mean, "Store up food and hide away in the mountains." No, thank God! John said, *When he shall appear, **we shall be like him;** for we shall see him as he is.*

How is Jesus? Jesus is victorious. He is more than a conqueror. Do *you* see Him as He is? He is seated at the right hand of the Father far above all principalities and powers and might and dominion. He has given us His name to use. Therefore, we are exalted with Him. When we understand that, *we will begin to be like Him!*

Revival of the Word

We are coming into a time unlike anything the world has known: a time in which God is going to manifest His power and His ability through men who recognize authority. Jesus is going to use the bodies of men. He will transport men through space in an instant of time to appear in other cities.

You will see these things in this generation! Jesus said He would make short work of righteousness on the earth. *We* are the generation that will see it. The greatest revival the world has ever known is already on the horizon. There are thousands of churches gathered in their little groups praying for God to send a revival. The last-day revival is the revival of God's Word. It is already here, but many have managed to avoid it through their religious tradition.

Listen to Jesus as He is praying in John 17:1-4:

These words spake Jesus, and lifted up his eyes to heaven, and said, Father, the hour is come; glorify thy Son, that thy Son also may glorify thee: as thou hast given him power over all flesh, that he should give eternal life to as many as thou hast given him.

*And this is life eternal, that they might know thee the only true God, and Jesus Christ, whom thou hast sent. I have glorified thee on the earth: **I have finished the work which thou gavest me to do.***

Notice that when Jesus said, "I have finished the work," we know that He had *not* finished the work. But I want you to catch something in the way He prayed and the way He talked—*He spoke the end results.* He never spoke what *was.* He never admitted death or defeat.

When Jesus raised Jairus' daughter, He put them all out and said, "Why are you bawling? She's not dead; she's sleeping." (Mark 6:39.)

Jesus was speaking the end results in His prayer to the Father: "It's already finished. I've already finished that which You called Me to do."

And now, O Father, glorify thou me with thine own self with the glory which I had with thee before the world was (v. 5).

You can see that Jesus was not the glorified Christ at this time. He was operating as a man anointed with the Holy Ghost; He was deity, but He was not operating in divine power.

God's Name

I have manifested thy name unto the men which thou gavest me out of the world (v. 6). There are seven names for God. One of them is **Jehovah-God**—"the covenant-making God." There is **El Shaddai**—"the Almighty One, the All-Sufficient One." Then there is **Jehovah-Rapha**—"the God that healeth thee."

Jesus said, "I have manifested Your name. I've manifested the God Who is *the covenant-making God.*"

For I have given unto them the words which thou gavest me; and they have received them, and have known surely that I came out from thee, and they have believed that thou didst send me. I pray for them: I pray not for the world, but for them which thou hast given me; for they are thine. And all mine are thine, and thine are mine; and I am glorified in them. And now I am no more in the world . . . (vv. 8-11).

Here is another of Jesus' statements: "I am no longer in the world." When Jesus said that, He was standing right there, and they were looking at Him. They didn't understand that kind of talk.

When He said, "I am no more in the world," He was talking the end results. He was using His faith and speaking His confession. *And now I am no more in the world, but these are in the world, and I come to thee. Holy Father, keep through thine own name . . .* (v. 11). (What is His own name? **Jehovah-Rapha**—the God that healeth thee.) *. . . those whom thou* *hast given me, that they may be one, as we are.*

Go through this whole chapter in your Bible and underline every place it says *as we are.*

While I was with them in the world, I kept them in thy name (Notice, He kept them in the Name: **Jehovah-Rapha; El Shaddai.**) *those that thou gavest me I have kept, and none of them is lost, but the son of perdition; that the scripture might be fulfilled. And now come I to thee; and these things I speak in the world, that they might have my joy fulfilled in themselves. I have given them thy word; and the world hath hated them, because they are not of the world, even as I am not of the world* (vv. 12-14).

Do you see what Jesus is saying? "There are unique people. They are not of this world, *even as I am not of this world*. They are people who have authority in the earth. Yes, they were born here legally; they have legal authority here. But they are going to be born again; they will be recreated. They will be supernatural men, men filled with the power of God and with the authority of a man, able to destroy the works of the Devil.''

I pray not that thou shouldest take them out of the world, but that thou shouldest keep them from the evil. They are not of the world, even as I am not of the world. Sanctify them through thy truth: thy word is truth. As thou hast sent me into the world, even so have I also sent them into the world (vv. 15-18). What did God send Jesus into the world to do? . . . *For this purpose the Son of God was manifested, that he might destroy the works of the devil* (1 John 3:8).

And for their sakes I sanctify myself, that they also might be sanctified through the truth (John 17:19). Someone suggested that He was just talking to the disciples and apostles. But then He said, *Neither pray I for these alone, but for them also which shall believe on me through their word* (v. 20).

That includes you and me. Every born-again Christian believes because of the words those men spoke. **He prayed this prayer for us:** *That they all may be one; as thou, Father, art in me, and I in thee, that they also may be one in us: that the world may believe that thou hast sent*

*me. And the glory which thou gavest me
I have given them* (vv. 21,22).

Hear what Jesus is saying: "Father,
the same glory that You have given Me,
I have given them." Those that believe
on His name are given the *same* glory.

*. . . that they also may be one in us:
that the world may believe that thou hast
sent me. And the glory which thou gavest
me I have given them; that they may be
one, even as we are one: I in them, and
thou in me, that they may be made perfect in
one; and that the world may know that thou
hast sent me, and hast loved them, as thou
hast loved me* (vv. 21-23).

Jesus was the Son of God, but He
operated as the Son of Man. He has
given *you* the same *authority*, the same
power, the same *ability*, and the same
Holy Ghost.

*Father, I will that they also, whom thou
hast given me, be with me where I am . . .*
(v. 24). Where was He? He was
standing in spiritual law above all
principalities, power, might, and
dominion. He was above the world
system. They will be *with me where I am;
that they may behold my glory, which thou
hast given me* (v. 24).

And I have declared unto them thy name, and will declare it: that the love wherewith thou hast loved me may be in them, and I in them (v. 26). In other words, "I have declared thy Name Jehovah-Rapha—the Lord that healeth thee—and I will continue to declare it."

He Will Declare That Name Through Believers

Jesus is seated at the right hand of the Father. How will He declare that Name? He is going to declare it through believers who are using the name of Jesus—**men anointed with the Holy Ghost using that Name.**

Do you begin to see the picture? Jesus will declare God's name through men anointed with the Holy Ghost. *They become one with Him.*

The prayer Paul prayed in Ephesians 3:14-21 brings greater revelation:

For this cause I bow my knees unto the Father of our Lord Jesus Christ, of whom the whole family in heaven and earth is named. (Notice, not one family in heaven and one in earth; but we are all *one* family.)

That he would grant you, according to the riches of his glory, to be strengthened with might by his spirit in the inner man; that Christ may dwell in your hearts by faith; that ye, being rooted and grounded in love, may be able to comprehend with all saints what is the breadth, and length, and depth, and height; and to know the love of Christ, which passeth knowledge, that ye might be filled with all the fulness of God.

Now unto him that is able to do exceeding abundantly above all that we ask or think, according to the power that worketh in us, unto him be glory in the church by Christ Jesus throughout all ages, world without end.

Man stands in the position of having authority in all three worlds, authority delegated by the Son of God. The glorified Christ delegated that authority to men in this earth. Yes, we can tap the heavens. We can go before the throne of God—*come boldly unto the throne of grace, that we may obtain . . .* (Heb. 4:16).

God has given Jesus *a name which is above every name: that at the name of Jesus every knee should bow*—of beings *in heaven,* beings *in earth,* and beings *under the earth!*

Every knee will bow to the name, **Jesus.** No name is greater.

He gave us His name. *Christ in you* is *the hope of glory* (Col. 2:27).

Unto Him be glory in the Church by Christ Jesus throughout all ages, **world without end.**

Charles Capps is a former farmer and land developer who travels throughout the United States, teaching and preaching the truths of God's Word. He shares from practical, first-hand experience how Christians can apply the Word to the circumstances of life and live victoriously.

He has authored several books, including the best-selling, *The Tongue, A Creative Force*. Charles also has a nationwide radio ministry called "Concepts of Faith."

Charles and his wife Peggy make their home in England, Arkansas. Both their daughters, Annette and Beverly, are involved in the ministry.

*For a free brochure of books
and tapes by Charles Capps, write:*

Charles Capps Ministries
*Box 69
England, AR 72046*

Books by Charles Capps

The Messenger of Satan

Jesus, Our Intercessor

Angels

The Tongue — A Creative Force

Releasing the Ability of God Through Prayer

Authority in Three Worlds

Changing the Seen and Shaping the Unseen

Can Your Faith Fail?

Faith and Confession

God's Creative Power Will Work for You
(also available in Spanish)

God's Creative Power for Healing

Success Motivation Through the Word

God's Image of You

Seedtime and Harvest

Hope — A Partner to Faith

How You Can Avoid Tragedy

Kicking Over Sacred Cows

Substance of Things

The Light of Life

How To Have Faith In Your Faith

Available at your local bookstore.

Harrison House
Tulsa, Oklahoma